Some Assembly Required:

A Networking Guide for Real Estate

by Chad Goldwasser and Thom Singer

New Year Publishing, LLC
Danville, California

Some Assembly Required:
A Networking Guide for Real Estate
by Chad Goldwasser and Thom Singer

Published by:

New Year Publishing, LLC

144 Diablo Ranch Ct.

Danville, CA 94506 USA

http://www.newyearpublishing.com

ISBN 978-0979988530 (Paperback)

ISBN 978-1935547006 (Hardcover)

Library of Congress Control Number: 2008935155

This book is dedicated to my wife for making me happy and cheerful always so I can be a great networker. And to the people that this book inspires to get out of their comfort zone and become magnets for business.

Chad Goldwasser

For Sara, Jackie and Kate, who make life worth living. And for my mother, a fantastic real estate agent. She taught me that people are important in all success.

Thom Singer

This book is dedicated to my wife for making me happy and cheerful always so I can be a great networker. And to the people that this book inspires to get out of their comfort zone and become magnets for business.

Chad Goldwasser

For Sara, Jackie and Kate, who make life worth living. And for my mother, a fantastic real estate agent. She taught me that people are important in all success.

Thom Singer

ACKNOWLEDGEMENTS

First and foremost, I must acknowledge my co-author Thom Singer for encouraging me to do this project; it has been a great experience. Not only are you a great friend, you are a great writing partner and you lift me up. I will always be grateful.

To my wife, thanks for giving me the time to work on this project amidst our busy lives. You are my greatest inspiration and my best friend. I will love you forever.

Thanks to my business partner Greg Cooper for manning the ship while I sat at my favorite coffee shop doing what I love: writing!

Thank you John Maxwell for inspiring me to write. Thanks to my kids for making me giggle and laugh. And thank you to my mother and my father, may you rest in peace Dad, for bringing me to this beautiful place called Earth.

Chad Goldwasser

I would like to thank Chad Goldwasser for his hard work and dedication to seeing this book across the finish line. As the third book in the *Some Assembly Required* series we were constantly under pressure to add value to the readers and expand upon the original *Some Assembly Required* book.

Special thanks go to Marny Lifshen, co-author of *Some Assembly Required: A Networking Guide for Women,* for her continued efforts to expand the franchise.

I am grateful to all the people who have passed through my life. My association with many amazing souls has allowed me to do the things I do today. To my family, which is more than understanding when it comes to the time commitment necessary to be an author and professional speaker, your support and love is always noticed and appreciated.

Thank you Dave and Leslie Morris at New Year Publishing. Leslie, our editor, helped take our thoughts and ideas and make them flow onto the page. Dave, as publisher, has continued to show by example the path to success that comes when you help others reach their dreams.

Thom Singer

CONTENTS

1 Networking as Part of Your Lead Generation Wheel 1

A successful career requires a network. 4

Take action and bust the myths 10

Four steps to building your network. 15

2 Getting Serious About Building Your Network 23

Getting your networking started 24

Build your brand. 26

Setting your networking goals. 31

Creating a plan. 35

Your network will not grow overnight 38

3 Architecting Your Plan 43

Shaping your vision 44

The strategy 46

Your Sphere of Influence 47

Identify your top clients. 51

Your target and wish list 55

4   Building Relationships Through Networking. 61

The process: managing a new relationship. 62

Scenario #1 63

Scenario #2 66

Tips for a successful one-on-one meeting 68

Gaining confidence and maintaining momentum. 73

The next level of networking 75

5   Organizations, Groups, and Events. 81

Types of organizations 82

Finding the right organizations 93

Be inclusive, attentive, and interested. 102

Visibility vs. credibility. 105

6   The Many Faces of Networking. 109

Creativity counts. 110

Utilizing your network to help others find work. 116

Some Networking Ideas for Women 117

Networking with an open mind 120

7   Your Toolbox: Tricks of the Trade 123

Tools for networking events 124

Follow-up tools 131

8   Mentors, Peer Groups, and Coaches 141
     What is a mentor? 142
     What is a coach? 149
     What is a peer group? 151

9   Networking Online 157
     What is online networking? 159
     Types of online networking 159
     Benefits of online networking for realtors 163
     Quantity vs. quality 165
     Staying safe online 167

10 The Finishing Touches:
     Turning Your Network into Real Business 171
     Getting the business 172
     Build internal support by sharing your network 173
     Never burn a bridge 175

     Conclusion: Making Networking Work for You 179
     Appendix: Recommended Reading 181
     About the authors 182

1

NETWORKING AS PART OF YOUR
LEAD GENERATION WHEEL

Imagine mountain biking in the picturesque Red Rock Mountains in Moab, Utah. It's 100° F outside and you're flying down the granite trail thinking, "It's a good thing the wheels on this bike are so strong; they take the brunt of the ups and downs, and the overall punishing nature of this environment."

This exact thought changed the way Chad viewed his business. He looked at the wheels on his bike and was amazed at their strength: the hub that holds it all together, the rim that holds the tube and tire, and the spokes that create the strong support system so the wheel does not collapse. For some reason, perhaps an infatuation with financial independence coupled with a drive to succeed in a big way, Chad started thinking about his own real estate business. What made his business strong? What was the foundation that got him through the ups and downs, the cliffs and the drop offs of a sales business. What were the spokes of his own personal business wheel?

It struck Chad that the difference was his ability to generate leads. From that day forward, he began to look at his business differently. He saw the way he generated leads as spokes that would allow him to create a stronger business. The more spokes that he had, the stronger his business would become and the higher level of financial success he would reach.

The bottom line in real estate sales is this: all things being equal, people will do business with people they know and like. Commission discounts can be matched, marketing can be matched, pricing can be matched, but a decade-long friendship and a mutual admiration cannot. This is one reason top agents make big money. Their long-standing client relationships bring in the deals. If a sales person moves to another firm, the business may very likely go with them. Chances are, if you have mastered the art of building strong relationships you will never have a lack of opportunities to list and sell homes.

The term "networking" is often overused, misused, and misunderstood. There are many different reasons to network and many different ways to do so; some ways are more effective than others. In real estate, the main reason you will build your network is to find people looking to buy or sell real estate. You will also utilize your network to find lenders, inspectors, title companies, builders, handymen, carpet cleaners, roofers, attorneys, and all of the other ancillary businesses that are needed to provide your clients with great service. The most successful agents also build a nationwide network of agents that can refer business back and forth when people relocate. Real estate sales provides an incredible opportunity to build a growing database of people that can, at no cost, advertise your services!

A successful career requires a network

In all industries, but especially in real estate, your network is your connection to future success. While having a great website, industry knowledge, collateral materials, business cards, a winning smile, and a firm hand shake are important, without a network you can never reach your full potential in the industry.

When Jean-Luc and his wife Kara were looking for a financial planner, they were referred to many professionals. They were overwhelmed with the number of choices. Ultimately they parted ways with the first person they engaged and began working with Mick Davis. Jean-Luc had met Mick at the gym, and they had been working out together for more than a year before he ever even considered engaging him professionally. Mick never pushed Jean-Luc to move their money (which was not much at the time), but continued to build a friendship. When it was time to make the change there was no doubt in the couple's mind to whom they would turn for financial planning advice. They now have referred several people to him and they are all happy clients. In turn, Mick has become one of Jean-Luc's best referral sources for his custom-designed jewelry, and they have a mutual understanding that each will help the other. This is networking. Having a network in the real estate business is not just about selling homes; it's about all aspects of your life.

What exactly *is* networking?

There is no right or wrong reason to network, as long as you understand what networking is, and what it is not. Effective networking is a way of life, not a sporadic strategy that is only followed when you need a buyer or seller! Think of it like dieting. People diet when they want to lose weight, and while they might succeed, the results are most often temporary. If, however, someone who wants to lose weight makes healthy eating and exercise a lifestyle, the results are far more likely to last. By the same token, agents who only network when they need new clients or are trying to find a new job will not enjoy long-term success.

Networking IS:

- A verb. It is an active, ongoing pursuit requiring a commitment.

- A process. The results are not immediate; it will take time and consistency for you to achieve your networking goals.

- An opportunity to break out of your shell and work on your speaking skills, which is great practice for open houses or when meeting with new clients.

- A way to meet interesting people and build strong friendships.

- A two-way street. You must be willing to help people and organizations as much, if not more, than they help you.

- An effort to build, maintain, and leverage mutually beneficial relationships.

- An opportunity to change your career and change your life.

- A lot of work, and also a lot of fun.

- The most cost-efficient and effective form of advertising.

- A great approach for expanding your thinking by meeting other high-production people.

Networking is NOT:

- A noun. While it is valuable to have a database of contacts, it is what you do with those contacts that counts.

- An occasional activity. It must be a part of your routine.

- Cold calling or sales. Real relationships cannot be built by phone or email, especially if they are one-sided. This does not mean that you cannot sell to people in your network; you just have to know the difference between selling and relationship building.

- Schmoozing or working a room. Events are excellent networking opportunities, and are just one small piece of the puzzle.

- A guarantee to improve your ability to list and sell homes.

- Rocket science. Anyone in real estate can improve their ability to build strong relationships through networking.

- Calling your past clients and asking them, "Do you know of anyone looking to buy or sell real estate?"

A network is having a lot of people who know and respect you, and understand your business. It is then easy for them to call on you if they need your product or service, or refer you to others because you are first in their mind when a need arises. By the same token, you understand their business and look for ways to send them work. A network is a give-and-take arrangement.

No one will do it for you

Networking cannot be delegated. Being a great networker and creating a powerful list of contacts that refer business year after year is up to you. Unfortunately many people do not realize that they must take ownership of this aspect of their career.

It is not easy to become a top-producing real estate agent. You must have a great ability to interact with and present to people, and you must prove yourself. If you sit back and wait for your friends and family to start referring you

business, you may be broke before you make your first
sale. Our friend Mario learned this the hard way. One of
his friends, whom he had worked with in a bar, was looking for a home. Just after Mario received his real estate
license he was helping this friend find a home, without the
friend committing to working just with him. In the end the
purchase was made through another agent. This happens
more often than you would like to believe because people
will still think of you in terms of your last job.

Thom's mother spent two decades at home raising Thom
and his brothers. When she joined the real estate profession after the boys were in school, she had to do more than
just announce she was now in the business. She not only
had to promote her services to her PTA friends, but also
had to get busy making connections with people whom
she would meet as part of her new profession. The mix of
educating those you already know, combined with forever
expanding your contacts, will lead you to success.

Look around your company. Are there people who have
stronger relationships with other agents, clients, or with
the management team? Very often those with natural in-
terpersonal skills excel faster than those who hide behind
closed office doors. The fact that you have opened this
book and have read these first few pages is a sign that you
believe in the power that other people can have on your
business. As you progress through these chapters you will
see that there is no magic bullet to propel you ahead. Your

career in real estate will span many decades and at no point will you be done networking. You will learn to build and maintain connections with other people and make it a way of life, not just something to do on days that you have some extra time.

Your Networking Quotient

Part of being able to improve your networking skills is acknowledging your strengths and weaknesses. Most people believe that great networkers were just born that way. This is simply not true.

To make strides in this area, you need to make a realistic assessment of your current skill level.

Tony Dungy, who led the Indianapolis Colts to their 2006 Super Bowl victory, said it this way:

> **"The first step toward creating an improved future is developing the ability to envision it. VISION will ignite the fire of passion that fuels our commitment to do whatever it takes to achieve excellence. Only vision allows us to transform dreams of greatness into the reality of achievement through human action. Our vision is what we become in life!**[1]

---

[1] Tony Dungy, *Quiet Strength*, pg 12.Tyndale House Publishing, 2007.

In conjunction with this book, New Year Publishing offers a free 33-question online quiz that allows you to assess your networking skills. By knowing where you stand today in regards to your abilities, you will be able to figure out how to take the next steps towards your mastery of this skill of networking. Taking this quiz will allow you to assess the best ways you can focus your energy for improvement. *www.nqquiz.com*

Take action and bust the myths

"There is no such thing as an overnight success. Every great company, every great brand and every great career was built in exactly the same way. Bit by bit, little by little and step by step. There is no magic solution for success."

Seth Godin

Myth 1: Networking is only for times you are not busy.

Reality: There seems to be a boom-or-bust mentality around networking. Some agents think that when business is good, they can ignore everyone around them, and that others will naturally understand that they are busy. Conversely, when things slow down, those people rally and try to pick up where they left off. They start calling past clients, their family, and their friends and asking who they know that is looking to buy or sell real estate. The problem with this methodology is that if you fail to cultivate relationships, they will wither away. Jumping in and out of networking, just like jumping in and out of prospecting, produces weaker results. No one is so busy that they cannot pick up the phone to get back in touch with others on occasion. You must schedule your calling time like it is a million-dollar cash buyer. And, since you have to eat lunch any-way, schedule it with someone that you want to see. If you are too busy to pay attention to other people then you are overworked, ineffective, or have an inflated view of your own importance. Stay in touch.

Real estate is a relationship business all of the time. Make networking a priority.

Myth 2: Networking is only important with buyers and sellers.

Reality: Networking benefits you when you spend time with current clients; however, you also need to continu-ously be making connections with others that may need your help. The most successful people we know be-come connectors. These high achievers do all they can to refer business to past clients, friends, and peers when they find people looking for those services.

Networking is a way for you to develop your inter-personal skills, identify potential employees or part-ners, connect with peers, and create new opportunities. Networking can also occur within your own company, helping to position you for the future. Look at it this way: your role as an agent within your brokerage may not be dependent on networking, but your goal of being a top producer does require you to work harder than the average person in all areas that can lead to success. A well-rounded agent's goal extends beyond helping people to buy and sell real estate (and then cashing the commission check). Instead, the well-rounded agent looks to positively impact the lives of others in their community and beyond.

Myth 3: Only the lead agent or rainmaker with a team needs a network.

Reality: If you have a team of people that works with you, everyone should be focused on expanding the visibility of the business. The senior agents should be teaching the younger agents and the administrative team how to cultivate relationships. Buyer agents, listing agents, and administrative assistants should have their own cards and keep their eyes and ears open for others to refer the team business.

If you are the kind of agent that sits back and waits for a lead to come your way like a little bird waiting to be fed, you will go hungry. You must produce your own business and show your community that you are more than just another real estate agent. No matter how much experience you have or what role you play in your company, affiliations with others who can and will refer you business is very important.

And remember, while networking, you are not only representing your team, you are representing yourself. If your employer won't support your networking efforts by giving you the time and resources to join organizations and attend meetings or conferences (shame on them!), find a way to make it happen on your own.

Myth 4: The people you meet networking never refer you business.

Reality: People refer business every day. Somewhere in your community a real estate professional is getting a lead right now. Why isn't it you?

A friend introduced Chad to Gary Manley, a local restaurateur. They quickly hit it off. At the time they met, Chad was recruiting sponsors for a charity concert. Gary quickly purchased two sponsorships but that's not the end of the story. A week after their initial conversation, having never personally worked with Chad, Gary referred a friend who was looking to purchase a home for his college-aged son. A month later the $450,000 sale closed.

This happens in the real estate business all the time. Do not fall prey to the myth that nobody ever refers business or that you will be left behind. Many times, however, the benefits of a relationship may not be as clear-cut as someone referring you a client. They become an advisor, a partner, a reference, or a friend. You may never even know of the favors they have done for you or your career. If you focus on finding ways to be a valuable resource for them, they likely will do the same for you.

Myth 5: Networking is unnecessary. If you are good to your clients and you have a good reputation, success will just come to you.

Reality: Many great agents struggle to make the number of sales needed to support their families. And not every client whom you serve will think to refer you, even when you did a great job. It takes more than just doing good work; people have to know about you and care about you. They need to understand that you are always looking for new business. Some people will hear of you because of the quality of your work alone, but if you are not actively helping advance your own brand, reputation, and network, many other people will not even know you exist.

Myth 6: You must be an extrovert to be a good networker.

Reality: Naturally sociable people may have the advantage of confidence and charisma, but networking is a set of skills that can be learned and developed. Everyone can succeed at networking if the right strategies and methods are consistently implemented, and if they practice. That's right; networking can be learned. Ask questions of those you meet and take an interest in their needs and challenges.

If large, stranger-filled events don't appeal to you, identify relevant organizations that host smaller meetings. Ask a successful agent if you can tag along with him or her. Or, focus on building relationships with key influencers one-on-one. If you are new to a job or community, join local clubs that address topics or hobbies that interest you. With time and practice, networking can become a comfortable part of your life.

Four steps to building your network

If you would like people to refer buyers and sellers to you on a monthly, weekly or even daily basis then you must make networking a big priority. Creating and developing business relationships can be fun, but is a process that takes effort. Attending a chamber of commerce dinner and wondering if it's the right group of people for you to meet is common. Do not try to prequalify everyone you meet. You never know when you will meet someone in need of your services, or who has a contact in need. Open yourself up to others and your networking will actually evolve quite naturally. It's important to not skip or rush through any steps.

Step 1: Introduce

The first step you must take is introducing yourself to a new contact at an event, in a meeting, through a mutual friend, or via phone or email. While this may seem straightforward enough, keep in mind that your actions during the introduction step of networking may well impact your future relationship.

The introduction is your one and only chance to make a positive first impression. Here are a few pointers:

- Greet people with eye contact, positive energy, a big smile, and a firm handshake. This also shows your confidence and professional appearance.

- Say your first and last name clearly, especially if they are unusual or difficult to pronounce. If you do not catch the name of the person you are meeting, ask them to repeat it immediately — it will save you embarrassment down the line. Repeat that name in your mind several times so you will remember it.

- Dress appropriately for the occasion. If you are unsure of what to wear, dress a little nicer than what you think is required, as it's always better to over dress than to under dress. Even if you work for yourself or have a flexible schedule that includes coaching your child's soccer team, dress professionally when showing up at networking events.

- Prepare for meetings. For example, if you are meeting with a potential vendor that a colleague has referred to you, research their products or services ahead of time. Know what they do and how you might be able to help them.

- Plan what you want to say if you are using email or the phone to introduce yourself. Be sure to state your purpose for contacting them. Don't fumble around with words, or be vague. We recommend using prepared scripts for every outbound call you make. This does not mean sounding canned and rehearsed; this means being natural because you have practiced your dialogue.

Step 2: Educate

The education step of networking is your chance to build a strong connection with a new contact, and making a connection is key. Your goal should be finding something out about that person that is important to them or that you have in common, and establishing rapport through that commonality. It is vitally important that you can talk about yourself effectively, and it is vitally important that you ask good questions and listen. Dig deep, find out more, and do not just ask to ask, ask to learn and know. It is not at all unusual for a couple of simple questions to completely stump people as they are chatting with someone at an event — common questions such as "What do you do?" or "What does your company do?" Develop solid and compelling answers to these questions. What differentiates you? What makes you special? Take time to figure those things out and rehearse your answers so that you are just as comfortable answering them as you are brushing your teeth.

It is important to remember that the education phase involves two people. Listen more than you talk; you have two ears and one mouth for a reason. The greatest conversationalists are often the ones that say the least. Often, people are trying so hard to make a positive first impression that they fail to learn about the other person. Asking creative, compelling questions, as well as talking a little about yourself, will lead you to natural links with others.

Connections with others are often built on a personal, not just a professional level. One of our favorite questions is, "What do you like to do for fun?" Great conversations often start with someone talking about their passions. Your most successful relationships will be with those that you discover you have common interests. The best business relationships are personal relationships.

Step 3: Follow Up

This is where the magic happens, the follow-up, and it is here that many agents stumble. Following up with new contacts takes both commitment and creativity. Sometimes it's clear how to follow up; for example, you agree to send a new contact information on buying or selling real estate. Sometimes, however, it is unclear how a relationship will evolve, and you may not know right away if or how you will be able to help one another. Keep these strategies in mind:

- Reach out promptly with an email, phone call, or handwritten note after initially meeting someone. They are most likely to remember you if you contact them within a few days of your first meeting. There doesn't have to be a reason for contacting them; getting in touch to say "it was nice to meet you" is enough.

- Do something to keep the connection alive and growing. With time and multiple interactions, you may well discover common ground or an opportunity to work together. If your company has a regular newsletter or e-letter, ask permission to add them to your distribution list. If you are hosting a relevant event, invite them. Keep them in the loop of what you are doing and ask them to do the same for you. Keep them in mind if you find someone in need of their service or product.

• Be creative as you seek ways to build relationships. Look for organizations, events, or newspaper articles that you think might interest that person, and pass the information along. If something newsworthy happens to that person or their company, send your congratulations; it shows that you are paying attention! When Thom published his first article in the *Austin Business Journal*, one of his contacts had the article framed and presented it to him as a gift. This simple gesture was greatly appreciated and the article has hung in Thom's office for over a decade. Each time Thom sees it he remembers the friend.

• Be prepared to let go. You will not have strong relationships with everyone. Not all people will become your friend or will refer you business. Sometimes there is no "click" or opportunities for follow-up don't present themselves. It's not personal; move on. Focus on where relationships are evolving.

Step 4: Maintain

Maintaining a relationship is the most important step. We all invest a lot of time and effort to seek out new contacts, but it is long-term relationships that serve us best over time. Sometimes people take for granted those that they know the best, and assume that they will be around to support them later. Continue to search for ways to add value to existing relationships. Study your database and your network and then reach out to your contacts so that you are always top of mind. Think about whom you can help and then do so when the opportunity arises. We know an agent, "Billy," who was surprised when his neighbor of seven years listed his home with another broker. While they had lived next door to each other, Billy had not done anything to cultivate the relationship. His neighbor had been golfing in a foursome with the other guy for a few months, and when it came time to list his home he felt closer to his new friend than he did to his next-door neighbor.

Additionally, we often assume that people will ask us for help if they need it, or let us know when they are looking to buy or sell real estate. Many real estate professionals have found out that a former client recently bought or sold real estate. When asked why they did not use their previous agent, clients will respond that they thought they were too busy or did not work in their geography. Ouch. Make sure that you are always educating others, and letting them know you can help. Toot your own horn; it is your responsibility to let the world know what you do. If they don't know, they cannot call you. Every relationship needs attention and focus. If you do not put in the effort to keep the friendship alive, one of your competitors will be happy to have the business. You do not want to lose an important ally due to negligence.

FAQ

How long does it take to build a strong network? It depends on how much effort you put into it. If you make it a priority, you will see results faster than someone who devotes half as much time to it. If you focus on others and direct business to them you will see results.

How do I become a better networker? Practice. Becoming a great networker does not happen overnight and if you want to get better at it, like anything else, you must practice. We suggest role playing with a trusted friend or group of friends. Start by working on your introduction and then come up with some key, common questions. Rehearsing will make you more comfortable when you get into the actual situation of talking with others at a networking event.

How do I know if I am meeting the right people? The more people you meet and connect with, the better your opportunity to generate referrals and build good relationships. This being said, we are strong believers in networking with high production people. These people, like yourself, just tend to have more opportunities to refer others.

2

GETTING SERIOUS ABOUT

BUILDING YOUR NETWORK

Building your network in your real estate business begins with your clients. If you've had any sales up to this point then this is where you need to start, as long as the people were happy with the transaction. How are you staying connected with those people? Are you following up with them? Many professionals cash their check and then move on to find new buyers or sellers. You need a plan to follow up with past clients for the rest of your real estate career and to become their realtor for life!

When you become intentional about your networking, you will come across many opportunities to interact with exciting and interesting people. Successful people build networks by cultivating true, long-lasting relationships. Building solid business relationships with people on foundations of less than genuine intentions just doesn't work. People either know and trust you, or they don't. Are you who you say you are? The greatest successes are people that attract others because of their consistent, authentic actions.

Getting your networking started

First, figure out where you are now. Are you a strong networker, aka a natural, or do you need help breaking out of your shell? Do you already have a system in place for keeping in touch or do you just leave it to chance encounters? Being honest is important, as it allows you to accept your strengths and weaknesses. If you find yourself wondering how to create mutually beneficial referral partnerships, then you are reading the right book.

Second, identify your networking goals. What do you expect from your network? As with any successful venture, you need a solid vision and clear goals, or you will wonder why you never receive any referrals.

Third, create your plan. Write down what it will take for you to create connections with people that will enable referrals to come to you every day. Build a system that is easy to follow. Be realistic about the time and effort that it will take.

Finally, hold yourself accountable. Keep your networking goals front and center so that you remember what you are working to accomplish. It's easy to get caught up in the process and lose sight of why you are networking in the first place. In other words, assess and build your personal brand, define your goals, create a solid plan, and evaluate your progress. Remember: you are not just seeking out relationships with other people for your own personal gain; a real network is mutually beneficial. Seek out ways to be a resource to others.

Build your brand

Your brand exists today. How do others view you? Do they think of great service? Reliability? Fun with boundless energy? Professionalism?

What do you want your brand to be? Give some serious thought to this before you begin to fine tune your public image. Chad envisions his company becoming the "Nordstrom" of the real estate industry, known for legendary service. His goal is for people to think that when they work with Goldwasser Real Estate, they will get the best agents and service that are available, period. The agent's individual brand and the company's brand jointly bring in referrals. Being conscious of your brand and tenacious in your maintenance of it are key to keeping your competition at bay.

Starbucks, Nike, Apple, and McDonald's have strong brands. They have name recognition and a stand-alone logo. Your opinions of these companies are based on the experiences that you and your friends have had with them, as much as by the advertising and public relations campaigns they run.

Corporations spend millions of dollars building and maintaining their brands. They seek feedback on their image and reputation from customers, vendors, partners, shareholders, and the general public. They do so because there is a quantifiable value to having a positive image; in fact, for some companies, their brand is their single most valuable asset.

So how does this relate to you? Each time you walk out the door you are putting that brand out there. Yet individuals often ignore the importance of managing their own brand. Your personal brand is your reputation, your image, your vibe. It is the impression you leave, the energy you give off, the way people talk about you.

Self-promotion in real estate is a large part of creating one's own personal brand. Many agents tread cautiously when mentioning their own accomplishments to avoid the perception that they are bragging. Some are equally reluctant to share their goals for fear of appearing too ambitious. In truth, there is a fine line between consistently communicating and demonstrating your strengths and being an obnoxious, self-centered promoter. However, if you don't let others know about your capabilities then you will get passed over for opportunities to become their agent of choice. The strategy of just doing a good job and hoping others will notice does not work today. Be compelling.

Ten things you can do to improve your personal brand

1. *Treat everyone you encounter with respect.* It is amazing how incredibly rude some people are. Treat your clients like gold and also give the same

treatment to lenders, title companies, inspectors, appraisers, and other agents. You never know where opportunities will come from.

2. *Dress appropriately.* Some agents wear jeans, t-shirts, sandals, and other clothes that do not convey professionalism. Dress for success. Your attire is a huge part of your brand, and some people are known for a specific aspect of their dress. There is a female agent in Austin known as the "Hat Lady." We are not suggesting that you wear a hat necessarily, but rather consider your dress as part of your brand.

3. *Volunteer.* Show your commitment to your community. The most successful agents give back. They support the local food bank or other charities that help those in need in their cities. Others donate a part of each commission to education programs. Create your giving routine from the get go. If you wait until you are wealthy to start writing checks, it might be difficult to pen large numbers, even if you have the money. Start small, be consistent and you won't miss the money while making a long-term impact on your community. If you give a little along your path to success, you will find that the small donations add up over time.

Additionally, participate in local business-oriented organizations. Your local chamber of commerce or other civic organization is a great way to volunteer your time while also meeting new people.

4. *Do a great job for your clients.* This should go without saying, but we have run across agents who love the business, except for the demanding buyers and sellers. Yikes! The people we serve in this industry are our purpose. You need to have commitment and integrity toward serving customers. Nothing else matters. Follow the Golden Rule. Do more for others than you would ever expect them to do for you! Follow through on what you promise, as too many agents say one thing and then do not deliver. Make stellar service your mantra.

5. *Mentor others.* Take other agents under your wing and help them learn the business. When you are in a transaction with an inexperienced agent, help them elevate their game. Too often, seasoned agents forget that they were once newcomers to the business. Look for ways to help others in the industry, as that helps the whole profession.

6. *Improve your public speaking skills.* As a real estate salesperson, you are interacting with potential buyers and sellers all the time. Becoming a great speaker allows you to present yourself in a more compelling way and keep your clients' attention as

you are working towards the close. You can also build your local reputation and brand by speaking at various events and to various organizations.

7. *Write.* Create articles for business or trade publications, and consider blogging. Positioning yourself as the expert in your area is one of the fastest ways to more business.

8. **Refer business to those in your network.** This is the most important thing you can do to build your reputation. Few real estate professionals make it a habit to give referrals. Become known in your community as one who looks for opportunities not just for yourself, but for others as well.

9. *Solicit feedback.* Ask the people in your network what they think of you. People may have reasons to not refer you opportunities. If you do not ask people about how they perceive you, you will never know if you are doing the right things. It's important to remember that everything you do and say is a part of your brand. Your actions are an integral part of how others perceive you. What's more, you cannot compartmentalize your personal life from your professional life. You will be judged for all that you do, good and bad. As a real estate agent, you must realize you are never given time off. Much like the paparazzi constantly view Hollywood celebrities,

your community is always watching your actions. Become the kind of person that people want to be around.

10. *Forgive Yourself.* We all make mistakes from time to time. Oftentimes people beat themselves up over their past, and that can keep you from moving forward to reaching your potential. Get a good therapist if necessary, forgive yourself, and move on. Other people are usually forgiving if they see that you have made necessary changes and do not repeat your mistakes. Be willing to do the same thing with yourself.

As with successful corporations, your personal brand is one of your most important assets, helping you to achieve your personal and professional goals. Embrace the opportunity to show the world why you're the best!

Setting your networking goals

How are you are going to network? Consider the following questions, and write down whatever comes to mind without prejudging your responses.

1. When I meet clients or potential networking partners, am I comfortable conversing with them?

2. What differentiated value do I bring to the table?

3. Who is the best-networked agent I know? What do I admire about this person?

4. Who are the five people I most want to meet to help my career?

5. What do I want to accomplish through networking?

After a day or two has passed, review your answers and make any additions that come to mind. With your notes close by, let's review how your responses can help you set networking goals.

1. *When I meet clients or potential networking partners, am I comfortable conversing with them?* When you are at an open house, speaking with a potential new listing client, or at a chamber of commerce dinner, is it easy for you to talk with people? Or do you find it difficult letting people know about you and what you do? We know an agent who can meet anyone anywhere and build immediate rapport. She always lets them know that she would love to help them when the time comes to buy or sell real estate. She is an amazingly un-shy woman with a flamboyant personality and people love her. She is genuine and she believes in what she does.

Meeting and getting to know new people is enjoyable for some and stressful for others. Not everyone is a social butterfly and often people who are more introverted discredit or ignore networking because it is not in their nature to mingle. If you naturally love social situations, great. Disliking social gatherings does not preclude you from being a successful networker. If this sounds like you, your first goal should be to just get out there. Determine a fixed number of events that you can handle in a month and force yourself to attend. You will be amazed at how much easier it is to network once the excuse of not attending the event in the first place is removed.

2. *What differentiated value do I bring to the table?* In your role as a real estate agent, you take something that is incredibly difficult and simplify it. What do you do that you can vocalize in a way that gets people interested in asking more? Maybe you are a neighborhood specialist, maybe you have specific certifications, maybe you have developed a proprietary system for marketing homes, maybe you work only with first time home buyers, maybe you specialize in Green homes, etc. Figure it out then write it down and practice saying it until you are very comfortable when it comes out of your mouth. Define your value, differentiate it, then articulate it. Once you know what you can do to help others, you can find ways to have an impact on your business community.

3. *Who is the best-networked agent I know? What do I admire about this person?* The person you have identified could become the greatest tool you have to expanding your own network. Call him or her and ask to get together. You will be developing a relationship with this individual that could evolve into something meaningful for you both. Building relationships with top agents is not only energizing, but sometimes it can lead to referrals, even in your own community.

4. *Who are the five people I most want to meet to help my career?* Maybe it's the head of human resources at a local company, the principal of your child's school, or the manager of another real estate company. Take the time to sit down and identify those people. This is not as hard as you might think. You may already know someone who can make an introduction. You could also approach them at a networking event. Take a chance; think of all the people who will *not* be doing the same thing. If the person is more difficult to contact, try reaching out by email, via an online networking site like *LinkedIn*, or by sending a good old-fashioned letter. Make it your goal to meet all five of these people in person, by phone, or via written correspondence within the next six months.

5. *What do I want to accomplish through networking?*
When you start making things happen and you
realize where you want to go, you will become
invigorated. Take a few minutes to write down how
your network will impact your life and how you
will affect the lives of others. If you are unhappy
with your current business and your network is not
producing results, this exercise can help you refocus.
Knowing what you want from your networking
efforts will make it easier for you to take proper
action.

Creating a plan

You're busy. You're building a company, meeting with buyers and sellers, closing sales, staying healthy, parenting and
being a good spouse, attending conventions, etc. The speed
at which we travel through this life is incredible. Where
does networking fit in? It's a challenge. The secret is to first
make networking a priority: commit to it, create a plan,
and finally, make it a habit and stick with it.

Build a mindset where networking is a key part of your
business. Put it on your To Do list and on your schedule!
Now take a deep breath and relax. Networking does not
have to take an inordinate amount of time as long as you
are smart about it.

If you are just starting out in networking or if your circumstances have changed, here is a basic plan that will work within even the tightest schedule:

1. Choose the one organization that is most relevant to your career or industry and be an active member. Most organizations only have one meeting per month, so commit to attend regularly. In real estate, you may choose the chamber of commerce, a local home builders association, or a Toastmasters group where you can not only network but also improve your presentation skills.

2. Hold meetings — coffee or lunch are fine — at least twice a month with important contacts. Study your database on a regular basis to be sure you are not overlooking important people. You don't have to have a specific agenda beyond building or maintaining your relationship.

3. Identify the two or three key annual events in your community to attend. It doesn't matter whether it's a black-tie dinner or a two-day real estate conference; figure out which events are critical and put them on your schedule.

4. Combine multiple meetings into one. If there are several people with whom you have been meaning to catch up with, consider scheduling one luncheon

with them all. If they don't already know each other, perhaps they should! Become a connector.

5. Contact two people in your network each week by email, phone, or handwritten notes. You don't have to be face-to-face to keep relationships intact.

6. Network online. These communities can be a great source of information, advice, and contacts, and nearly every profession and industry has one (See Chapter 9 for more on online networking). Additionally, this can be done outside of traditional business hours, which helps free up your daytime schedule.

It is better to fully commit to a limited number of activities than to sporadically participate in many. Set goals that are realistic, then hold yourself accountable. Try to involve your friends or colleagues in your networking; if you arrange to meet up with someone at an event, or join an organization with a colleague, you will be more likely to follow through.

While making a commitment to networking may seem daunting, it really is quite manageable once it becomes a habit. Keeping in touch with happy, satisfied former clients is essential for you to receive referrals, but also reaching out to people you don't already see or talk to on a regular basis will help tremendously.

Tracking, evaluating, and revising your networking plan

Regularly evaluate your plan to make sure it's delivering the results you want. Is your network growing? Are you receiving more referrals? Are your past clients raving about you? These are all questions you should be asking when evaluating your networking plan.

The benefits of networking may seem intangible at times, which is why evaluating your results will help keep you motivated. Keep your database current. When you attend an event and meet new people, get their names into the database promptly, along with notes about them, potential opportunities, and how you might follow up with them. If you learn about a promising group to join or think of an idea for an article or speech that may be helpful to your network, record these as well. It will help you actually follow up while tracking which events and organizations are giving you the best contacts.

Your network will not grow overnight

One of the most common mistakes that people make in networking is having unrealistic expectations about when they will see results. Relationships are developed over time as rapport and trust are built. The people we meet do not run back to their office and search their databases for leads to send to us. Opportunities to help people sometimes do not present themselves for months or even years. Be patient, be consistent, and stay focused on the big picture. Build relationships strong and deep to see results.

You may also want to categorize the people in your network. A person that refers you on a regular basis is an A. People that refer once in a while are Bs. People that do not refer often are Cs. Evaluate how the people in your network are helping you, and evaluate how you are helping them. Make sure that you are spending time letting your As and Bs know how much you appreciate them. With your Cs, continue to educate them on how they can refer and learn about how you can help them.

Each of us only has a certain amount of time to invest in building relationships, and while we want to be polite to everyone, there are people who never give anything in return. Learn to identify these people. If you find yourself sending a lot of business to someone or assisting them regularly and they tend to be too busy to reciprocate, focus your energy elsewhere.

Take time to plan and put effort into thinking about your networking. Referrals do not just happen. Become intentional about building your referral base and over time you will be encouraged in your abilities to build a strong network.

FAQ

What do I say when I phone a client that I have not spoken to in a long time? For a lot of people this is hard to do. Don't beat yourself up, just dial. Try this:

> "Hi Joe, this is Kevin Sinclair with Capital City Real Estate. It has been way too long. I have done a poor job keeping in touch, haven't I? Are you still loving your home?"

This will work. Just be honest and get the conversation started. Remember what people like to talk about: themselves. Use the F.O.R.D. technique. Ask about their Family, Occupation, Recreation, and Dreams.

How can I be a resource for my network? Let people know that if they ever have any questions about real estate, they can call you. For instance, one strategy is to send out a letter letting those in your network know that you are an expert in tax appraisal issues.

Do you have a large library of self improvement books, learning CDs, or other training materials? Invite people to borrow them. You can also buy copies of your favorite books and send them out as referral thank-you's or as follow-ups to great meetings.

How do I figure out my brand? Take time away from your business, at a local coffee shop perhaps, to sort this out. Write down your ideas and brainstorm, then refine until you come up with a solid idea. This may feel like non-productive time, but it's not. Taking time away from working in your business to work on your business is essential.

How can I increase my service levels? You have the ability to change the way that people look at our industry. Focus on your professionalism, your market knowledge, your return call time, your attention to detail and your systems to increase your service levels. The biggest complaint that people have about agents is their lack of communication. This is one small area that you can focus on, but there is so much more. We suggest getting your Certified Residential Specialist designation, Graduate Realtor Institute, Accredited Buyer Representative, or other high-level educational certification. Doing this will make you more focused on client service.

How do I track my results? Develop a system for incoming leads so that you can send thank-you notes and gifts as appropriate. You can use an Excel spreadsheet or database software. However you do it, don't underestimate the necessity of it. Help yourself by recognizing who it is that is referring you and make sure they know how much it means to you.

3

ARCHITECTING YOUR PLAN

Many real estate agents get out of bed each day and utilize the "hope and pray" method of building their business. They hope that someone calls to buy a home and they pray that one of their listings sells. The truth is, almost anyone can be successful in the real estate business. The hard part is the work.

People often wonder how a successful agent can sell 500 homes in a year. It's very simple: hard work. You get up in the morning and do the things that generate sales. A lot of well-educated, seemingly ambitious people have given little thought to what they need to do to get more from their business, and instead, proceed through their career without a vision.

To succeed, you need to see the goal and put together the steps. To be a top producer in real estate, you need to decide where you are going and then do the specific activities that will get you there. You need to plan your work and work your plan.

Shaping your vision

Do you see yourself as having a successful future? That is the first step. Begin by thinking about what your future will look like. Envision your business as thriving and growing, and start shaping that vision for a better tomorrow.

Take control of your attitude about your own success. This will help pull you forward toward achieving your goals. Vision is the ability to see a better tomorrow. Vision will give you hope, it will ignite the fire within you, it will keep you working hard. It will pull you through the inevitable tough times and it will give you a reason to get out of bed and execute the plans that will enable you to reach the end goal.

Schedule a day for yourself. Maybe start with a brisk walk, get some air in your lungs, and really wake up. Go to your favorite breakfast place and think about what you want out of life. Using a notebook is an easy way to make sure that these ideas do not get lost.

Once your mind is in gear, just start writing. Create a story, a perfect picture for your life. What does it look like? What does it feel like? What does it taste like? Smell like? What is it that you want out of your business and your life if no limits were to exist? Create that. Now read through it and get excited. There is something about seeing the words on paper that makes it more possible, more plausible.

"Look at things not as they are, but as they can be. Visualization adds value to everything. A big thinker always visualizes what can be done in the future. He isn't stuck with the present."[2]

---

[2] David J. Schwartz *The Magic of Thinking Big*, pg 155. Simon and Shuster, 1969, Prentice Hall

Don't get stuck in the present; start thinking bigger about your future and about your network.

The strategy

Would you encourage someone to build a house without a set of blueprints? Imagine what that home would look like. No matter how good the materials and the builder's intentions were, it would still be a disaster.

Your plan is really just the simple steps that you will take to realize your vision. They are your blueprint. Your plan allows you to make sure you have all the pieces in place to accomplish the project. When building a home, for example, you would need to know where the plumbing was to be located before the foundation was poured. You would know if that house would have one story or two. You would need to know how many bedrooms it would include. All of the little details would be spelled out in advance.

It is the same thing with your business. Without knowing how other people in your network can influence your career, you will miss many opportunities. Opportunities come from people, so neglecting to make networking part of your plan means missing potential sales.

Your Sphere of Influence

Your Sphere of Influence is made up of all the people you know: friends, family, co-workers, neighbors, clients, past clients, former co-workers, etc. It's all the people that you see on a daily, weekly, and monthly basis that may be able to refer you buyers and sellers. So, whom do you know?

It's interesting to see agents who say they really do not have a network. Hogwash! You know a lot of people already, even if you have never formally considered the reach of your network. It's important to know who is in your Sphere of Influence, and how you will get to know them better and cultivate a more mutually beneficial relationship.

To get a grasp on the current state of your network, put down on paper the names of those who have touched your life. This is your first step to creating your network, and it's the first step in your networking plan. For this process we have given you a memory jogger that we use to get us thinking about whom we know.

Memory Jogger

Your list of prospects will be your most powerful tool on the road to success and financial freedom. Below is a list of types of people and trigger words to help trigger your memory.

Accountant

Advertising

Aerobics

Airlines

Antiques

Apartments

Architect

Athletics

Attorney

Auctioneer

Auditor

Automobile

Band / Orchestra

Banking

Banquets

Babysitters

Baseball

Barber

Basketball

Bible School

Bicycles

Billiards

Boats

Bookkeeping

Bowling

Boys' / Girls' Clubs

Broadcasting

Builders

Buses

Butchers

Camping

Caretakers

Carpet Cleaning

Cellular Phones

Cemeteries

Chiropractors

Church

Cleaners

Close Friends / Associates

Clubs

Collection

Colleges

Computers

Consulting

Contractors

Copying

Cosmetics

Couriers

Crafts

Credit Union

Cruises

Day Care

Deliveries

Dentists

Dermatologist

Designers

Detectives

Diaper Service

Disk Jockey

Doctors

Driving Ranges

Dry Cleaners

Dry Wall
Electrician
Engineering
Entertainment
Eye Care
Family Members
Farming
Fax Equipment
Firemen
Fishermen
Florists
Food Service
Fund Raising
Furniture
Gardens
Gift Shops
Golfing
Government
Graphic Arts
Grocery Stores
Gymnastics
Hair / Nail Salon
Handyman
Hardware
Health Clubs
Health Insurance
Hiking
Horses
Hospitals
Hotels

Hunting
Ice Skating
Jeweler
Judo / Karate
Labor Unions
Leasing
Libraries
Mail / Mail Order
Management
Manufacturing
Mechanics
Military Personnel
Mobile Homes
Modeling
Mortgages
Past Associates
Pets
Photography
Publishers
Real Estate
Security Systems
Sheriffs
Social Services
Stocks and Bonds
Surveyors
Teachers
Title Companies
Training
Vendors
Volunteers

With this process, do not limit yourself, thinking that some people would not do business with you. If you make the effort to get to know them better and be a resource for them, most people will look for ways to return the favor.

Let's consider your dentist. Who is he or she? Do you see them on a semi-annual basis? Do they have a family? Do they own real estate? Do you know who they work with for their own real estate needs? Have they ever referred a friend or co-worker to other vendors they work with? Have you ever referred someone to them? This is a perfect example of someone in your Sphere of Influence with whom you can build a great referral relationship. In this process, remember to break through your reservations and try to become the Go-To Person. The more people you know, the better the chances that you will forge strong relationships with those who do like to help others.

Choose these people wisely. After all, you only have 24 hours in your day and you want to use them effectively. One of the most common mistakes that agents make in attempting to build their network is thinking that it's solely a numbers game. While anyone can refer you business, not everyone will. In the end you still need to be strategic in the kinds of people with whom you are looking to build your network.

"Experience will not save you in hard times, nor will hard work or talent. If you need a job, money, advice, help, hope, or a means to make a sale, there's only one surefire, fail-safe place to find them — within your extended circle of friends and associates."[3]

Identify your top clients

Once you have created your Sphere of Influence list, it's time to find your Champions. This is the second simple step in your plan. Your champions are those people that have referred you at least once in the past year. Don't worry if you can only identify a few of these; it's your starting point, and you will work hard to develop more of these people. Can you identify a dozen? After listing your champions, jot down a few bullets about how you first met them. If they were a client, make notes about how they found you originally. Why do they continue to refer you? Finally, do you think that any of these people has a need for a new property? If so, call them, thank them for being a great client and find out if they would be interested in either of these options, or if they know of anyone looking to buy or sell real estate. Staying connected is the only way to keep your relationship alive.

---

[3] Keith Ferrazzi, *Never Eat Alone*, pg 21. Broadway Business, 1st edition, February 22, 2005

Murray helped a couple buy a home. Within a month of that purchase, Murray did a follow-up call with them to see how things were going and ask if they would be interested in investing in a small rental home. They said they would, and three weeks later Murray helped them to close on their first investment property. The story does not end there. A month after that, their college-aged daughter needed a home and Murray got the call. Three sales took place within three months with the same people because Murray was proactive. Do you think these people are champions for Murray? Absolutely.

Champions are the kind of people that are thrilled to work with you and will consistently tell others about you. They are so enamored with you that they feel that people will be harmed if they work with any other real estate agent. Imagine having a dozen of these people running around spreading your good name.

> "The biggest asset is off the balance sheet — it's our loyal associates and our loyal clients. Without them a business has nothing. Few business people understand and act as if their customers are the biggest asset."[4]

---

[4] Jack Mitchell, *Hug Your Customers*, pg 206. Hyperion Books, 2003

Identify your advocates

Let's go back to your Sphere of Influence list and identify your Advocates. These are the people that have referred you at least once. They know you and trust you. These are the people that you want to move to the champion level by finding out how you can help them. You need to build a mutually beneficial relationship, where both parties are enjoying the connection and benefitting from it.

Steve is Charlie's advocate. They met in a father-son camping group. They did not know each other very well, but Charlie had made an effort to get to know Steve better. On one weekend campout, Charlie mentioned to Steve that if he ever knew of anyone looking to buy or sell real estate, he would be glad to help.

"As a matter of fact I do," said Steve. "My neighbors are thinking of moving. I'll talk to them about you and email you their contact info."

This was exactly what Charlie had hoped for. If Charlie had not said those few words, Steve never could have known to make the introduction. The neighbors began working with Charlie. Steve felt great about making the referral, and Charlie wanted to build on that so he invited him to lunch so that he could find out more about Steve, and how he could help him in his business. It turned into a mutual referral relationship.

This is how your Sphere of Influence turns into real business opportunities. It will become a constant fertilization ground for you to build and develop strong relationships that will produce opportunities. You will get to know the people in this group so that you are always on the lookout for people to refer to them. The more you know about them, the better your chance to find ways to help them, and the better your chance to discover similar interests and experiences that will help you solidify your friendship. This is how you grow a strong referral base. Being a connector means you match people that may benefit each other even if there is no apparent benefit to you.

The rest of your list

While champions and advocates are where you will build the bulk of your referral network, don't forget about the rest of the people you know — they can still do business with you when they are in need. Continue to market and send items of value to these people; when they are ready to buy or sell real estate they will reach out to you. They may not be grabbing people by the shirt and screaming your name at the top of their lungs, but you need them just as much as you need those champions.

Having a large database pays long-term dividends. We know that we are looking for buyers and sellers all of the time and this last group can be a strong source for those leads. This group is made up of past clients, current clients, neighbors, friends, family, business partners, and people that you do business with such as your banker, your dry cleaner, your doctor, your attorney — essentially anyone that you know and like and who feels the same about you.

Once you have identified these groups and entered them into your database, you are on your way. Now make it work for you. It is amazing how many buyers and sellers cannot even recall the name of the agent who helped them. Do not become a victim of your inability to keep in contact. Take control of your database.

Your target and wish list

The last step in this process is to identify a target and a wish list. Who are the people that you would like to get to know? Is it first-time homebuyers or high-net-income individuals? Is it a certain demographic such as golfers or senior citizens? Your target list is simply a specific group to target once you get into the marketing aspect of this whole networking puzzle. Your wish list consists of people that would be great connectors, people that someday it would be great to have in your network.

Chad's goal was to develop relationships with highly influential people. While attending a silent auction, he bid on and won a lunch with the mayor of Austin. Sometimes it

---

SPHERE OF INFLUENCE
Everyone you know, all the people that you see on a daily, weekly, and monthly basis.

CHAMPIONS
People that have referred you at least once in the past year. They know how to help other people make the decision to work with you and they do.

ADVOCATES
People that have referred you at least once. They know you and trust you.

---

will take unorthodox methods to meet people who you believe will have an impact on you and your life. When you are looking for ways to meet people, keep an open mind.

Your contact strategy

Now that you have identified your list of contacts, you need a strategy for contacting them. We call this strategy a Lifetime Connection Program. This is a series of emails, phone calls, personal notes, gifts, invites to parties, lunch dates, updates on the market, and other items of value that you will continue to deliver for the entire lifetime of your relationship.

For your Lifetime Connection Program to work, you must be sure that you have current, relevant information about the people in your network. The more you know, the more meaningful you can make your contact. For example, if you know that Casey is an avid golfer, you can invite him to the local golf tournament instead of sending him tickets to the opera. You want to make sure that every time you contact people it is for a relevant reason and that you have more to discuss than just their ability to send you business, although you always want to mention that!

Systematize it

This is an easy item to miss. If you create a system for delivery of your messages that is solid, you will win. If you do not, it will be tough to keep up. When you have a hundred or more people that you are keeping in contact with, it is tough to make it all happen if you are not prompted to do so. We would suggest implementing a customer relationship management software program into your business now to help you keep up with your growing network. Examples of these are Top Producer 8i, Salesforce.com and Plans Plus Online. Find one that you like and use it, as it will allow you to become more organized in your effort.

Stick to your plan

Leaving your relationships to chance is gambling with your career. Have a plan that keeps you focused on the power of your network. Many professionals assume that since they are a good-natured people, their business relationships will take care of themselves. While this is true with a small Sphere of Influence, to be successful you need to expand your network all the time. Be deliberate. Many people never invested time to really consider and systematize their networking efforts. Have you?

FAQ

I am just not a visionary person; how can I create a solid vision? There are many people who feel that they are not "visionary." We all have vision though, and it may just take a little time for you to develop yours. Go back to the first part of this chapter and take the time to write a story about your life. Make it as vivid and as perfect as you possibly can. You may want to make it a little outrageous and stretch your imagination. Consider a perfect, limitless life. Push yourself and don't hold back.

What should I consider when adding to my sphere of influence? In a nutshell, find people that you click with. Also look for people that fit the demographics of your current clientele, or if you are looking to change your market then look for people that fit into that niche. Again, it's good to add all people that you have a relationship with or that you meet to your network, but it is best to focus your energy on people that do a lot of business like you and will have the opportunity to refer you.

What should I do for my champions? Everything and anything. Take care of them and build strong relationships and friendships with them, and do it not just for the business. Do it because life is all about good relations. Refer them business, and send them thank-you notes and gift cards to somewhere they like every time they refer. Take them to ball games or ballets. Attend their parties when you are invited, learn about them, treat them like gold, and let them know how much it means to you that they refer.

I have people in my database that I do not remember. Do I just delete them? It happens. Here is the script we suggest, and while it may sound a little out there, it works:

> **"Hello Jim, this is Stuart Brock at Brock Real Estate and I feel totally silly making this call, but you are someone that I have in my database and I cannot for the life of me remember how we know each other. Have we worked together in the past?"**

One of two things will happen; they will either laugh, tell you how you know each other, and re-establish the connection, or they will tell you to get lost, in which case you clean your database. Simple.

4

BUILDING RELATIONSHIPS
THROUGH NETWORKING

Have you ever gone into an appointment with a home seller and asked them who helped them buy their home, only to find out that they cannot remember the agent's name? This is all too common. Real estate professionals are most often very transactional in their behavior and do not focus on the long-term relationship after the sale. It's not enough to just know people; one of the most important steps of networking involves staying in touch.

To establish the necessary trust that's needed to identify opportunities to help one another and gain referrals, you'll need to know more about your clients and your networking partners than is found on a business card. This requires a creative and consistent effort of discovery, both immediately after meeting someone, and once you've established a rapport. Focus on finding the things that you have in common, and on creating a shared history of experiences, rather than on what you hope to reap from the relationship. View your database as a warehouse of information about the people that you know, and study it. Create time in your schedule to know your network and refer to them.

The process: managing a new relationship

Once you have begun to implement your networking plan, you'll meet new people, make important contacts, and close deals. Exactly how do you manage and develop these new relationships so that they can become mutually beneficial connections? How can you build a strong referral network among your current and past clients, as well as your Sphere of Influence?

Fortunately, the process can be made easy. The following suggestions are meant to be a guide; as with everything in networking, you'll need to make adjustments for your own situation and comfort level.

Here are two scenarios:

Scenario #1

Miriam is an agent with Davis-Hill Real Estate, and she is having lunch with an executive recruiter with whom she has a successful referral relationship. During lunch, the recruiter runs into Greg, one of his clients, the CEO of a growing biotech company. He introduces Greg to Miriam, and during their brief conversation Greg mentions that his company expects to relocate 15 or 20 employees locally by the end of the year. All of these people are going to need to find homes, right? Here is one follow-up strategy for Miriam:

TASK	TIMELINE
Research Greg thoroughly. Google him. Read his company's website. Ask the recruiter for his insight. Ask co-workers what they know about the company. Utilize industry sources for additional information.	Prior to contacting Greg
Initiate contact with Greg. A personal phone call or snail-mailed packet will have more impact than an email. Remind Greg how they met, referring to the recruiter by name, and directly state the specific reason for the contact. Ask for a face-to-face meeting.	Within 2-3 days of the introduction
Schedule a meeting. Do this at Greg's office at a date and time convenient for him.	1-2 weeks in advance
Confirm meeting.	48 hours prior to the meeting

TASK	TIMELINE
Prepare materials. These are personalized for Greg, demonstrating Miriam's knowledge of his company and industry. Practice presentation.	Prior to the meeting
Arrive for meeting 5-10 minutes early. Allow some time to build rapport with Greg before segueing into the presentation.	The day of the meeting
Send a thoughtful, handwritten thank-you note.	Within 48 hours
Send a follow-up letter with any additional information requested during meeting.	Within one week
Ask for the business. This can be done subtly (i.e. "I'd appreciate the opportunity to work together") but it must be done. Continue to contact and build rapport in a non-annoying manner.	During the meeting, and in all follow-up materials

Scenario #2

George is an agent with Phelan Realty and lives in the Horse Acres subdivision. At a neighborhood block party he meets Skip, another neighbor, and they chat for a while about sports, careers, and their kids. Skip casually mentions that he thinks that his neighbor might be moving soon. George says that he would love to help him and Skip says he will see what he can do to refer him. Here is one way George can follow up with Skip without just hoping the referral takes place:

TASK	TIMELINE
Drop off Home Sellers Guide. George should let Skip know before he leaves the neighborhood gathering that he will drop off information that Skip can give to the neighbor.	Within 24 hours after returning home
Send Skip a handwritten note. George should tell Skip how much he enjoyed getting to know him and how he appreciated the referral to his neighbor. In the note include a small gift card from the coffee shop.	Within 48 hours

TASK	TIMELINE
Once the referral is received, George makes sure to take great care of it. He should call Skip, thank him, and give him an update on how it is going.	Ongoing
Make lunch plans with Skip to find out more about Skip's work and to further build the relationship. Set the time at a restaurant of his choice and at a time convenient for him; also let him know it is your treat, a thank-you lunch.	Within 2 weeks of receiving the referral
Brainstorm on ways to help Skip, personally or professionally, and make this offer. George never knows where he might be of assistance, and simply extending the offer will make a positive impression. Listen attentively to what Skip's hobbies and interest are. Maybe he is a sports fan and can be invited to a game, or a golf nut that you can enjoy a round with. Transfer all of this information to database upon returning to the office.	At lunch and ongoing

Having a list of specific tasks with deadlines will help you ensure that networking opportunities do not slip away, and that referrals are handled appropriately. It's easy to be enthusiastic in the early stages of building a new relationship, and it's also easy to lose momentum as time goes by. Put a follow-up plan in your database to ensure you do the right thing.

Tips for a successful one-on-one meeting

One-on-one meetings are the best way to build and maintain relationships with important contacts. While you can't focus your entire networking strategy on spending solo time with others, you should view every personal meeting as a precious gift. There are only 24 hours in a day (and you need to sleep, too), so any time that someone agrees to sit down with you is golden.

Meetings give you the chance to:

- Spend quality, focused time together without the distractions of larger gatherings
- Learn more about someone and their business, and tell them about you
- Privately address specific topics or explore potential opportunities
- Strengthen your connection and build trust

People who go into networking meetings without a second thought as to their goals are missing an opportunity. While you may not have a specific agenda for every meeting, always have a purpose and a plan so that the meeting is relevant and valuable for you both. Always remember also that the greatest conversationalists are the greatest listeners!

There are four things to be when attending any kind of meeting:

1. Prepared

2. Respectful

3. Attentive

4. Focused

Below are some tips for conducting successful meetings:

- **Prepare.** And then prepare some more. Do your research so you can speak intelligently about the company and person you are meeting. The Internet makes it easy to do basic research, and your knowledge will make a good impression. Also, bring a notebook and use it.

- **Meet according to their schedule and offer to go to their location.** Make the meeting as convenient for the other person as possible. If you are the one requesting the meeting, this is proper etiquette. If a person tells you that a certain time is best for them, make it work for you.

- **Arrive on time and leave on schedule.** Time is a precious commodity. The best way to demonstrate your appreciation for the appointment is to arrive and depart on time. Real estate agents are notorious for showing up late. Buck the trend. Always predetermine the length of the meeting and confirm it when you arrive.

- **Be respectful of their priorities, requests, and comfort zone.** People tend to talk first about the things that are on their mind the most. Let them dwell on that topic, even if it's not what you most want to discuss. Be cognizant of what they want to talk about and do your best to listen and add value.

- **Watch their body language.** You can tell a lot about a person by paying attention to their body language. If they appear distracted or in a hurry, don't dawdle. If, on the other hand, they appear intrigued by a certain topic, stay with it until they're ready to move on. If they become very animated while discussing another aspect of their business, zone in on that.

- **Do more listening than talking.** This can be hard, especially for extroverts. Ask open-ended questions to draw people out; this is how you will learn about their priorities and concerns. Asking questions not only gives you critical information, but also it demonstrates your interest in them and makes them feel important.

- **Combine professional and personal conversations.** You now know that some of the strongest business connections are initiated through personal connections and vice versa. Invest the time to find the things you have in common, and allow the friendship to take root. Learn about their family, their background, their hobbies, their interests. Do it in a way that is not contrived.

- **Take notes.** As mentioned previously, this is another way to make your companion feel important. It is thoughtful, however, to ask the other person if they mind you taking a few notes. Your notes will also give you something to refer to regarding next steps.

- **Summarize what you have heard.** A brief run-down of the key points you discussed during your conversation is an effective way to end a meeting. This is especially true if you agreed upon specific action items. Reiterating and clarifying these items before you leave will make follow up much easier.

- **Ask for what you want.** Be sure you get what you came for. Your goal for the meeting might be to brainstorm on new client sources. It might be to voice your interest in joining the board of an organization. Whatever it is, make sure you do not leave the meeting without making the ask!

- **Ask if there is anything specific you can do for them.** Make sure that they understand that you want this relationship to be a two-way street. Let them know that you will help them in their business.

- **Confirm next steps.** It is common for two people to leave an upbeat, enjoyable meeting with no idea of what comes next. Sometimes the next step is obvious, such as providing a referral to a colleague, sending a proposal, forwarding information on an event, or arranging a second meeting. In more general "get to know you" meetings, the next step may be unclear, so take the initiative to suggest one, even if it's just to get together again in a month or two.

While many of these tips seem to be most appropriate for sales professionals, they apply to most types of professional social interaction. More informal meetings can take place over breakfast, lunch, or happy hour and it may not feel right to whip out your pen and start taking notes. Still, you should use strategic planning and proper etiquette to ensure a good use of time for both you and your companion. Also, if you can become a master of taking mental notes and putting them into your database, people will be amazed at your powers of recollection when you talk with them in the future.

Gaining confidence and maintaining momentum

As networking becomes more and more a part of your life, these techniques will become more natural for you. Try to break out of your comfort zone and move to the next level of consciousness.

Some people are impatient to see the tangible windfalls of their networking. Don't be one of these people; remember that Rome was not built in a day. Invest the time to transform casual contacts into a network that can be your most valuable asset.

Keep these things in mind as you build relationships:

People do business with people they know and like. While a lot of factors are weighed into a buying decision — price, quality, reliability, fees, marketing — all other things being equal, buyers and sellers will choose the agent that they have the best feelings about. In a world where more products and services are being commoditized, having the advantage of being well known and well liked is critical.

Consistent efforts with multiple contacts are the key to success. The concept is simple: don't put all your eggs in one basket! While you do need to be strategic, strive to network with people in a variety of environments. You must remember that it is up to you to become known to a variety of people in your business community. Networking is an ongoing task, one not to be turned on and off like your sprinklers are seasonally. Divide your networking time between building and maintaining existing relationships, and creating and developing new ones.

No one can network for you. You cannot delegate networking to your business partner. As much as it may be a task that you would rather ignore, you are the only one who can build your own reputation and image. Have some fun with it. Become a magnet for people with your smile and your positive energy!

People with magnetic personalities were not born that way. While it is easy to assume that these outgoing people are just wired differently, it does not always come naturally. With determination and practice, everyone can become more charismatic. Take a look at the list of our favorite business books in the Appendix. People like to spend time with those who are self confident and are focused on others.

Your network is bigger than you think. Do you feel like the only people in your network are the ones you know personally? In reality, your network includes not only those people, but also all the people in their networks. Likewise, their networks actually include everyone in yours. Consider social networking tools. You just need to let people know what type of contacts you have, and what contacts you are looking to make. A network is healthy when everyone helps each other. Many people do this every day by calling friends to find a good housekeeper or asking their neighbor whom they hired to paint their house. Extend this practice to your professional life.

The next level of networking

Once you have gotten into your groove, look for new ways to make contacts. Consider these:

Network with your competition. Instead of viewing your competition as the enemy, consider the reasons you should know them:

Critical information: You can be assured that in conversations with clients, prospects, and other influencers, the names of your competitors will come up. It's in your best interest to know them, and their strengths and weaknesses. Knowing your competition takes some of the fear out of competing with them, and will prepare you to respond appropriately. For example, if they are the market leader in a neighborhood, if they are offering a new system for selling, or if they provide deep discounts you will know what's coming, and you can practice answers to objections.

Potential leads: It's common in many industries to gain leads from your competitors when they are unable to take on the business themselves. For example, Chad had a good relationship with another agent in Austin. That agent, who was just leaving on a month-long vacation, had a potential listing coming up so she called Chad. For a small referral fee he took on the listing. This can also happen with expired listings, as the outgoing agent very well could tell his friends about the opportunity.

Also, some agents specialize in certain geographic areas of a city, and refer clients to others who work in different neighborhoods to ensure the clients receive the highest level of service. In doing so, the agent makes a good impression with the client by saving them a lot of time and effort in finding the right representation.

> **"People don't refer you because you meet minimum expectations. They refer you because they expect you to do a good job, which enhances their relationship with the person they are referring."** [5]

Finding talent: As your own company grows and you need to find new employees or agents, you can tap into

---

[5] Dr. Ivan Misner, *Truth or Delusion?: Busting Networking's Biggest Myths,* pg 5, Thomas Nelson, October 17, 2006.

your network. If you already know your competition, then you probably know who its superstars are. You will know who has the right personality, skills, experience, and work ethic to thrive in your organization. This simple networking strategy can make the hunt for key people much easier, saving you time and money.

Future employment: Similarly, it is not uncommon for other companies to look to their competition when opportunities arise within their organization. If you are visible to your competition, and have a good reputation, you could easily make the short list for upward career moves.

Become a Go-To Person. Having a solid network makes you more valuable. People turn to you when they need information, not because they think you know everything or everyone, but because they know that you will know where to find the answer. Why would you want to be a Go-To Person? You might find it bothersome to frequently have people contact you with random inquiries. In reality, it depends on how you look at it. Is it an effort to answer a call or email, and then think about whom to direct the person to? Of course. But, if one of your goals is to make yourself first in the mind of others in your community then you've succeeded. And you will certainly gain the appreciation, trust, and loyalty of those you've helped.

Go-To Person cannot be selfish. Do not look at inquiries as a hassle; look at them as an opportunity. If you know someone who has a need, and you know another who provides that service or product, make the introduction without concern for what you get out of the deal. Be mindful, however, about simply providing information, not an actual reference, unless you have personal experience with the person or company you are referring. You may someday be held accountable for the performance of that company; unless you make it clear you are providing an introduction and not making a recommendation.

> **"The behavior that best creates credibility and inspires trust is acting in the best interest of others."**[6]

Open your network to others. Once a quarter, look at your database and give some thought to those who would benefit from knowing each other. Here are two easy ways to do this:

1. Pick out five people whom you know well and search for those it would be mutually beneficial for them to know.

2. Pick out the five newest additions to your network and see whom you can introduce them to.

---

[6] Stephen M.R. Covey, *The Speed of Trust,* pg 81. Simon and Schuster, November 6, 2006, Paperback

Either way, make it a habit of linking up people in person, or through an introductory phone call or email. Everyone wins when you do this.

FAQ

Is it okay for me to talk shop at the neighborhood block party? By all means! Don't talk just about work but definitely talk to people about what you do and more importantly, find out what they do. To become the agent of choice in your neighborhood, you have to get the word out.

How do I get people to open up and tell me who they know is looking to buy or sell real estate? People don't just volunteer this information so it's imperative that you gain their trust by sharing your knowledge and expertise. Once you do this, and people really see you as the expert, they will refer people to you.

How do I develop my own follow-up plans for my network? Your plans do not have to be elaborate. When things are simple, you will more readily follow them. Pick specific things such as writing personal notes, phone call, lunches, or having coffee. Then add in some more time-intensive activities such as riding bikes or boating, taking people to concerts. Be sure to keep your plans in your contact management software and automate them so that you don't forget any of these appointments.

How do I remember what I've said to whom? Write it down or commit it to memory until you get back to your database. Focus on the people that you are with and do not allow yourself to daydream, and you will find you pick up a lot more about the people in your network. When you learn a lot about others and they watch you retain it, they will think more of you and you will build a stronger connection.

I am new to town. How do I get started? Starting a real estate career in a town where you do not know anyone is going to take significant effort on your part. You will have to get out more, spend more time meeting people, and build connections quicker than if you had a healthy Sphere of Influence.

What is the best strategy for becoming the "Go-To" agent? Strive to build your knowledge and your network. You should be studying, taking classes, and waking up every day with the goal of improving your skills as a real estate expert and expanding your network.

FREE EBOOK DOWNLOAD

go to www.newyearpublishing.com/realestate to download a free eBook version of the book.

5

ORGANIZATIONS, GROUPS,

AND EVENTS

Joining organizations and attending events are two efficient ways to build, expand, and maintain your network.
Organizations give you the opportunity to regularly meet
and interact with people, and to connect with those who
have similar interests. The best organizations offer events,
educational programs, volunteer and leadership opportunities, and additional resources to members such as books,
educational CDs, and newsletters.

Attending large events is also an efficient method of
networking, due to the sheer number of people who participate. While there are times that a one-on-one meeting is
the most appropriate strategy, attending events will bring
you in contact with many potential contacts. When your
time is constrained, events enable you to meet multiple
people, renew acquaintances, and build relationships, all in
a short amount of time.

Opportunities come from people. Therefore, if you're
avoiding contact with other people, you are avoiding your
future business deals.

Types of organizations

There are countless real estate organizations that you can
join. However, branching out from industry-related groups
is a good strategy. Others in the industry may not need to
engage your services, while those in the general population
will be buyers and sellers at some point. Do some research

to determine which groups are the right fit for you. Participate in the organizations that you believe will have the most benefit.

Make sure that the groups you are evaluating will help you to attain your networking goals. As with networking, membership is a two-way street. You will need to be able to contribute to the organization, as well as benefit from it. Committing your time to these types of organizations can be amazingly worthwhile as you become the go-to person for real estate information. However, if people find you unreliable, it can backfire, so make you sure you are willing to get involved.

As you consider membership to different groups or organizations, ask yourself:

1. What do I hope to gain from joining this organization?

2. What do I hope to bring to this group?

3. Is this association the best use of my time and energy?

4. Will this organization help me achieve my networking goals?

If you can't clearly articulate the answers to these questions then you have additional research to do. Consider groups that add to your personal development as well as offer ways to meet others. Combining personal growth and education with networking is a great use of time.

People who join groups that they are not interested in will quickly stop attending. If your local symphony has a powerful professional auxiliary group but you hate music, do not select this group just for the contacts you could make. If you do not enjoy the activity, you will either not attend the group events, or be clearly agitated while present.

Here are a few types of organizations to consider:

National and local boards of realtors

It is essential for a realtor to be an active member of the National Association of Realtors. NAR can offer you information and events like no other group. Attending the annual NAR conference is an excellent way to expand your reach nationally as you meet agents from all around the country that can refer you business. Building a national network of agents that you can mastermind with and refer business to is a smart way to generate sales.

Your local board of realtors is an absolute must as well. Being an upstanding member of your local board is good on many levels. First, there are lots of opportunities for education and events. Local boards have been around a long time; Thom's mother was an active participant in the Arcadia Board of Realtors in Arcadia, California more than three decades ago. Today the power of the local boards is even greater.

Additionally, being a member of your local board of realtors will grow your reputation with others in your community. It will give you opportunities to interact with peers, be part of the leadership that creates policy, and be exposed to best practices.

One agent we know benefitted greatly from her membership and participation with the local board:

> **"Another agent's listing was about to expire. We became friendly through our membership at the Austin Board of Realtors and he called me to see if I would be willing to list the home. I did, and sold it quickly. He was happy because he earned a referral fee, the client was happy because their home sold, and I was happy because I got a paycheck and built two great relationships, one with the agent, the other with the seller."**

Being a member of your local board comes with big benefits. Being a member of these organizations will show people that you are a dedicated professional.

Educational groups

In real estate, there are unlimited opportunities to align yourself with like-minded individuals. By obtaining designations from CRS (Certified Residential Specialists), GRI (Graduate Realtor Institute), ABR (Accredited Buyer Representative), LHMS (Luxury Home Marketing Specialists), or any of the other hundreds of designations now available, you will align yourself with top-producing agents. Surrounding yourself with agents that want to be the best will lead you to individuals from whom you can both learn the most and mutually refer business.

One agent we know is still reaping the benefits of earning his CRS designation. He told Thom:

> "I remember going to Las Vegas to get my CRS designation. It was a six-day course. During that time I built relationships with ten top agents from around the country. We formed a mastermind group and had monthly phone calls for two years. The phone calls stopped but the referrals haven't. In the nine years since that course I have received over 25 referrals, and I have sent out well over 25 myself. The relationships are still going strong and I am amazed at the level that these agents have grown to."

There are hundreds of real estate training programs and trainers; Howard Brinton, Mike Ferry, Brian Buffini, and Joe Stumpf are just a few. Getting involved with these types of training groups creates even more opportunities to learn key skills and build relationships that will allow you to grow your network.

Business organizations / chambers of commerce

Many business organizations function on a local or regional level. They often address the needs of an entire geographic business community, or a particular issue within that community such as transportation infrastructure or workforce retention. Organizations sometimes focus on a particular segment of the business community that crosses industries and professions, such as women or young professionals. Membership in these organizations is especially beneficial because they offer access to a wide variety of professionals and a diversity of events.

If you do not know which types of organizations exist in your city, or you do not know how to get involved, ask other business owners for recommendations.

Community and social organizations

Community and social organizations provide local opportunities to serve. Rotary International is one well-known group, as are the Jaycees, Kiwanis and Elks. Clubs built around common interests such as reading, snowshoeing, or knitting can help you build your network. Active group participation provides you with an opportunity to establish relationships with people you might not otherwise meet.

Charitable organizations

Charitable organizations often draw upon local business leaders to volunteer on their boards. If you want to make connections with these people then roll up your sleeves and dig in. Volunteering is an excellent way to network with a variety of people within your community while serving a worthy cause. However, before you donate your time, be sure that you have a real commitment to the cause. If you are not honestly interested in the charity your time spent with it will be painful and you will not succeed in building genuine relationships.

Chad's own cause is Rock and Restock, an annual concert that benefits Austin's Capital Area Food Bank. Over time, Chad has become passionate about his community's need for ongoing support of their food banks and he invites his friends, family, and client base to this event every year in an effort to make a difference.

Thom has created a giving endowment to the Dell Children's Medical Foundation in Austin. A percentage of his speaking fees goes to a research program for children born with cranio-facial abnormalities. Through this program, he has had the opportunity to meet several of the hospital's board members and other volunteers, and expand his network.

Giving back is the right thing to do. When you do something to help others, it comes back to you. Do not just look at philanthropic activities as a way to generate business; give with no expectation of anything in return. We have found that getting involved in this aspect of your community brings with it a wonderful sense of satisfaction that goes beyond looking for the next sale. However, anytime you encounter new people with whom you share common goals, you will uncover more opportunities.

If you need help selecting a charitable organization, go to www.volunteermatch.org. This website helps potential volunteers clarify their interests and skills, and then matches them with a local charity in need.

Family participation

Involvement in line with your family interests is another way to network. Coaching for your child's soccer team or volunteering as an elementary school room parent will expose you to other parents. These activities will bring you into situations where you will interact with people in casual, meaningful ways. In Austin there's a neighborhood group called Adventure Kids and Dads which is an informal collection of about 40 dads with elementary-school-aged children. Each month the group goes hiking, canoeing, jet skiing, bowling, etc. Participants get quality time with their children and expand their networks.

University alumni organizations

University alumni groups can be one of the most natural networking experiences, as all members immediately have one thing in common — their alma mater. The same can be said about sorority or fraternity alumni associations. If you were a member of a sorority or a fraternity in college and have not joined its local alumni group, you are missing a huge networking opportunity! Sisters and brothers are generally more than willing to help each other, and can be a great way to find a mentor. These groups often hold regional or national conferences, which offer excellent networking. They can be especially helpful if you have just moved to a new community. Alumni groups often hold social events and organize volunteer projects — and you'll have a leg up in getting involved in your new community.

Toastmasters

Public speaking is often cited as the number one thing most feared by Americans. Death ranks number two. If this rings a bell, we have two words for you: Toastmasters International.

Everyone should participate in a Toastmasters group at some point in their life. The group is dedicated to helping people in all walks of life improve their public speaking skills. For those who work in real estate, this is a must. Better presenters win more business and have greater opportunities to expand their personal brand.

We have both been active members of Toastmasters for over a decade and are still amazed by how many people have never heard of the organization, which has been around since 1924. Its charter reads: "Through participation in the Toastmasters Communication and Leadership Program, people from all backgrounds learn to effectively speak, conduct a meeting, manage a department or business, lead, delegate, and motivate." These are all skills that can help you in your real estate business.

There are Toastmasters clubs in every major US metropolitan area and in 80 countries. Many people who are familiar with the organization have never looked into it because they think the clubs are made up only of advanced speakers. To begin with, you will benefit from enhancing your public speaking skills, regardless of your industry or job function. Clubs are made up of people with a variety of speaking skills. Joining Toastmasters is the smartest career move either of us have made. We have had countless experiences where we've been called upon to address a crowd, formally or informally, and we never could have succeeded in such talks without the skills that we have fine-tuned through Toastmasters.

In addition, many people have actually made business connections from people they met within Toastmasters. People have met future employers and employees because they are exposed to people who are focused on personal growth, and often find like-minded others.

You can find all the information you need at www.toastmasters.org.

Toastmasters International
PO Box 9052
Mission Viejo, CA 92690 USA
Tel: (949) 858-8255

Finding the right organizations

How can you find the organizations that will enable you to be a contributing, involved member while also providing you with access to relevant people?

1. *Ask your peers.* Find out where your industry colleagues are involved. Talk to other agents in your community as well as in other communities to find out what is working for them. Talk to your friends as well, even if they aren't in your same industry, geography, or stage of life. If they can't give you a specific recommendation, they may know someone who can.

2. *Search the web.* You may have to play around with searches and review multiple websites to find relevant information, but the information is out there and in great quantity.

3. *Attend an event.* Talk to members about the benefits they find from their involvement. See what attending an event is like and if you fit in. Ask members how they felt about this program as compared with past events. While speaking to people, be sure to ask what their level of involvement with the organization is, as someone who attends events only occasionally may be less enthusiastic than a committed member.

Leveraging your involvement

Remember that organizations are simply a vehicle for you to further develop your knowledge, skills, reputation, and network. Your role in the organization is just as important as the organization itself. Just becoming a member will give you few direct benefits; you will get out of it what you put into it. How can you make the most of the time and money you spend in membership?

Take advantage of the benefits of membership. Reading a monthly newsletter or scanning the organization's website will not give you much ROI. Benefits will vary greatly from organization to organization, ranging from continuing education to health insurance and singles' groups. If the organization offers events or conferences, attend as many as are relevant to you. Regularly reading the organization's newsletter will let you know who the movers and shakers are, and give you an idea of whom to seek out while at events.

Be a leader. Organizations are rife with members that just pay their dues, attend occasional events, and add the name of the organization to their resume under "Community Activities." What most organizations really need are volunteer leaders, those members who step up and do the work required to keep the group functioning. Volunteer for committees, including the non-glamorous roles like staffing the sign-in table at events or taking minutes at board meetings. Serving on committees enables you to build your skills and experience. If, for example, you want to gain more confidence in sales, fund-raising would be a good choice for you.

> When our friend Grace decided to take on the role of president of her Rotary Club, it was daunting. Although she did not know if she was totally qualified to do it, she left fear aside and did it anyway. What Grace found was that it gave her more exposure, did not take too many hours of her time, and the benefits were numerous. In the year that she was president the group thrived and increased membership. She was viewed as a good officer and it has served her leadership skills and personal brand well.

Work the roster. Without a doubt, the single biggest advantage to joining an organization is your fellow members. They will be a resource for ideas, contacts, advice, and camaraderie. Within the membership ranks are referral sources, clients, friends, partners, mentors, and future employees. It is relatively easy to build relationships with other members since you will interact regularly. Be careful not to cross the line between networking and sales, however, as it may make other members uncomfortable. Many groups have rules against soliciting the membership for your own business purposes. However, once you have made a connection with someone, use your best judgment on how to discuss your real estate business. Most people are willing to listen to business presentations from people they know, but they might resent your assumption that just because you are a member of the same group you can call them. Get to know people first. When you are asked what you do professionally make sure that you are knowledgeable about your market so that you can impress people.

Know when to move on. Not every organization is appropriate for lifetime membership. You may find that your involvement in an organization has run its course. Don't be afraid to move on. It may be hard to let go, especially if you have served in a leadership role and have long-standing friendships within the group. If you are serving on the board, limit your service to three years. You do not want to be the person who begins each meeting with a history lesson of how the board acted in years past. If the organization is still a good enough fit for you to remain involved, drop off of the board and give others an opportunity to contribute.

Making the most of events

When most people think about a networking event, they envision a crowd milling around a hotel banquet room with cocktails in one hand and business cards in the other. However, there are almost as many types of networking events as there are networking organizations. Events range from breakfast meetings with a dozen people, to speaker luncheons with 100 attendees, to black tie dinners with more than 1,000 attendees. Each can be a valuable experience if you make the most of the opportunity.

As with joining organizations, attending events is only effective if you do so with a plan. Ask yourself, "What do I hope to gain from attending?" The more tangible your answer is, the more likely you are to see results. For example, if you are a member of the hosting organization, your goal may be to network with other members. Perhaps the event is featuring a guest speaker on a topic that is interesting to you personally. Or, the event might offer you access to a particular group of people that you would like to meet. The important thing is to attend with that benefit firmly in mind.

If you are not sure why you are going to an event, or how you hope to benefit, or if your heart just isn't in it, your time is better spent elsewhere. Many people show up to events late, sit by themselves, speak only to people they know, and then sneak out early. This is an example of what not to do. These people go home thinking, "Well, that event was a waste of time," when actually it was a wasted opportunity.

There are several strategies you can use to ensure that attending an event is a good investment:

Research the event or host prior to attending. When attending an event, be knowledgeable about both the event and the host. The Internet makes this simple. This information will make it easier for you to engage in conversation, so take a few moments to become familiar with the host organization, the guest speaker and topic, or the criteria for an awards program.

Attend with a colleague. There are several advantages to attending an event with a colleague, the least of which is that you are not on your own. If you are new to networking or are an introvert, it can be especially comforting to know that someone is right there with you. They can give you a landing point if you find yourself wandering the room alone or in between conversations. Attending with a colleague also gives you twice as many opportunities to meet people because you can meet the people your colleague already knows.

Invite clients, prospects, and referral sources to attend with you. Events are an easy place to multi-task. If you are planning to attend an event, ask yourself who might be interested in attending as well. This can be an extraordinarily good use of your time — not only will you be spending time networking, you'll also be with someone important to your business. It's nice if you can pay for them, but if not, it is still okay to invite them along. Just make sure that they are aware of the cost so that you do not end up with an awkward situation.

Arrive early for the best networking. There is no question that the best networking is at the beginning of an event — regardless of whether the event is in the morning, at lunch, or in the evening. Attendees will be in a rush to get to the office or go home as soon as the event is over so if you are hoping to connect with someone, do it first thing. Since many events feature a speaker or program that will limit your time to network, arrive early to interact with other attendees before taking a seat. Also, upon arriving, you can scan the table of pre-printed nametags to see who will be there. It is also easier to walk into an empty room than it is to try to join 200 people who are already engaged in discussion. When you arrive early, it is as if the others join your party instead of you struggling to get up to speed.

Spend your time both initiating new relationships and building existing ones. It is easy to arrive at an event, see a friend or professional contact, and spend your time catching up with them. But you must also commit to meeting new people and initiating new relationships, even though this can be a bit more intimidating. Aim to meet three to five new people at each event and to make a good connection with them. If you keep this goal in mind, you will be conscious of the time you spend talking with any one person.

Use strategic seating. Your networking does not have to stop when you take your seat. People tend to sit with people they already know. Instead, try sitting next to someone you haven't met. There will probably be a few minutes to chat with your tablemates prior to the start of the program, so make good use of this time. Be sure to exchange business cards before you leave the table. You can also purchase or reserve tables at key events, and invite people to either attend as your guest or reimburse you for seats at your table.

Follow up within three days of an event. Follow-up is the most neglected aspect of networking, even though it's the most important. We've all met someone at an event, had a good conversation and made a connection, exchanged business cards, meant to schedule a follow-up meeting or send them information, then somehow let it slip through the cracks. Prompt follow-up can make or break a new relationship. Make it a priority and a habit.

Event etiquette

There is quite a bit of etiquette involved in attending events, and yes, people do notice. You want to make sure to come across as professional, polished, and confident. Here's a refresher:

Be prepared to introduce yourself, colleagues, and guests. The most common error people make while at events involves introductions. People either don't introduce themselves or don't introduce the people that they are with. This creates an awkward moment. It is especially common when a group of people in conversation are joined by someone new. It is proper etiquette to introduce the newcomer to everyone in the group as soon as they join you. Try to include first and last names, their company or profession (if appropriate), and an idea of how you know each other. An example of this type of introduction is:

> **"Marcus, I'd like you to meet Albert Wong, an agent with Wu Wei Real Estate Partners. Albert, this is Marcus Walters, an appraiser I've worked with on many sales."**

Respect quiet time. When a networking event has moved into a meeting with a program or a guest speaker, it's time to be quiet, regardless of how engaged you are in conversation. Respect the speaker by paying attention. If someone tries to engage you in conversation at an inappropriate time, smile, nod, and then break eye contact, returning your attention to the speaker. If they persist, you may have to tell them (quietly and respectfully, of course) that you would like to listen to the speaker. Good manners and respectful behavior are always noticed, as are their negative counterparts.

Silence your cell phone, pager, or PDA. These devices have been a great help to networking in many ways and they have also created some etiquette challenges. Whether you are in a one-on-one meeting, mingling at an event, or listening to a panel of experts, there is no acceptable time to answer a call, return a page, or read/send a text message unless you are a physician and you are on call. Real estate agents are massive culprits in this type of behavior and we must stop. There is no such thing as a real estate emergency. By exhibiting this kind of behavior you are telling the people you are with that they are not as important as the call/page/email that has diverted your attention. Many people have fallen into the habit of utilizing these tools anytime, anywhere. If you catch yourself doing it, stop!

Be inclusive, attentive, and interested.

Are you an *Excluder?* At events there are often small, tight groups of people that seem impenetrable and may intimidate you so much that you won't approach them. They may actually be reminiscent of high school cliques! Strive to be the opposite, including and welcoming people into your conversations. Networking is, by definition, an inclusive activity, and events are a perfect place to expand your circle of contacts.

Are you a *Scanner?* There are also people who constantly scan the room, looking to see who else is there. While you might think this is a good networking practice, it is actually rude if you do it while in conversation with someone. It gives them the impression that you are looking for someone better to talk to, and may also leave them feeling like you're not listening to them. Give all of your focus and positive energy to the person you are talking to, and you'll both get more from the interaction.

Are you an **Egomaniac?** It's easy to dominate conversations without even being aware of it. Realtors love to talk about themselves. Listen more than you talk. Not only is this good for you in networking, it is also great practice for when you are speaking with a buyer or seller. If you need to divert the focus to someone else, or need to restart a conversation that may have hit a natural lull, try a few of these questions:

1. What do you do?

2. What does your company do?

3. What are the biggest current challenges in your job/ company/industry?

4. What's the best part of your job?

5. How are you connected to (name of organization hosting the event)?

6. Are you involved with any organizations or charitable causes?

7. What is fun or exciting in your life right now?

Always RSVP, arrive on time, and leave early only with great discretion. Realtors are notorious for being late. Don't be! This boils down to respecting the event's host and attendees. RSVPs are critical as they enable the event's organizers to plan for the appropriate amount of food, beverages, seats, nametags, and so on. It will reflect badly on you if you attend without RSVPing, just as it will if you RSVP but do not attend. Arriving on time is the most professional thing to do, while arriving late will draw unwelcome attention to you. If you must leave an event early, slip out discreetly at an appropriate time, such as between speakers or when the wait staff is clearing dishes. If you know ahead of time that you will have to leave a seated event early, sit close to an exit. And, of course, bid your tablemates farewell as you depart, letting them know why you must leave early lest they think they have driven you away.

"You can make more friends in two months by becoming interested in other people than you can in two years by trying to get other people interested in you."[7]

---

[7] Dale Carnegie, *The Leader in You*, pg 5, Pocket Publishing, May 1995.

Visibility vs. credibility

One of the perks that come with active participation in organizations and events is raising your visibility. There are also pitfalls if you do not act appropriately. Anyone can be visible — if you are in enough places often enough, people will begin to recognize you, and your name will become known. Being credible, however, is a higher level of recognition where your expertise, integrity, and influence develop into a positive reputation.

How can you create the right kind of visibility while developing credibility?

Participate only in relevant organizations and events. Focus your participation on things that make sense for your business and personal interests, rather than simply trying to be in as many places as possible. You don't want people trying to figure out why a real estate agent is attending a meeting of dental hygienists.

Follow through with your commitments. If you take on any kind of a volunteer role, be sure to deliver what you promised. Only commit to those activities you know you have the time and ability to accomplish. Following through is equally important when offering to help people, whether by introducing them to a potential client, helping them find a job, or by passing on the contact information of a great babysitter. People will remember whether you kept your word.

Develop relationships, not contacts. This is a classic case of quantity versus quality. If a large number of people have heard of you and perhaps even met you once or twice, this constitutes visibility. If a smaller number of people personally know you, can speak to your unique capabilities, and will serve as an advocate for you, this constitutes credibility. Focus on developing relationships and trust with key individuals, within key organizations, and at key events, rather than using mass marketing techniques.

Many people become well known and well liked, but that alone will not get them much. To be famous without substance is basically useless, both personally and professionally. Experience, ethics, hard work, and commitment provide credibility, which is of real value.

FAQ

How much money should I budget for joining organizations and attending networking events? It depends on which you join. Toastmasters, for example, has a minimal expense, approximately $40 a year. Chamber of commerce memberships can range from hundreds of dollars a year to thousands, depending on the size of your company. A membership to your local board of realtors runs $600-$700 and membership in the National Association of Realtors is extended to you with membership in your local board. Groups that are not networking focused, such as a running club or a scrapbooking group, may be things you'd belong to regardless of your career interests, and can very well be a great source of new relationships. These may be free or have very minimal costs.

How much time should I expect to invest in being a member of an organization or attending events on a monthly basis?
Again, it depends on how much you participate in. Remember this: the time that you put in will be proportionate to what you get out. People that just show up once in a while will not get as much out as those that are heavily involved. A networking group will meet, on average, once a week or once a month, for an hour. Being involved in your local board of realtors will bring you lots of opportunities for education and leadership. Classes can be anywhere from a half day to several days depending on the level. If you become president of your local board, your time commitment will be great. NAR is a little different; attending the national convention is a great way to be involved and it spans four days.

We suggest having a plan for your time spent networking so you do not end up spending all of your time networking and none of your time actually doing the business that comes from networking. Make sure that your family understands the importance of the time you invest in networking. Thom and his wife have agreed on a maximum of two nights a week he will be home late, and on Sunday they review the calendar to make sure that everyone, kids included, knows the schedule.

How can I build relationships with agents from around the country? Do not make the mistake of believing that if you go around and hand out business cards, or set information on seats in conference room, that you are building your national referral network. The process of developing relationships with agents in other states is a lot like the process of building your local network, the major difference being that you will not be able to take these people out to lunch or invite them over to your house for dinner on any sort of regular basis. But, you have to pay the same special attention to them that you do to your local network. Keep information that you learn about them in your database. Learn about their interests, their families, their goals, and their dream. Send them personal notes, call them and, most of all, do your best to refer them business. Create a follow-up plan specifically for out-of-town agents.

How do I find out about events that might be good for me to attend? The Internet is one such place. So is your newspaper's business section. Also, find out where the people in your network are going and see if you can tag along.

6

THE MANY FACES OF NETWORKING

As you know, networking takes many forms and serves many purposes. While it takes consistent effort and creativity to truly reap the benefits of networking, it also can become a comfortable, natural part of your real estate career. In fact, you're probably networking even when you don't realize it! Serve as a connector, finding opportunities and making introductions, even if it will not directly benefit you. The best networkers help others without regard to the payout, and in turn, they are repaid in countless ways.

Creativity counts

It is easy to follow the leader. You frequently see this in industry marketing; agents advertise where their competitors advertise, assuming that it works well. Everyone has been doing the same things for years: magnets, recipe cards, just sold/just listed cards.

What will you do to differentiate yourself? It's a better strategy to be unique even though it requires more effort. After all, new and unusual ideas get more attention.

Consider holiday cards. How many of the cards that you received last year from businesses had laser-printed labels and lacked a personal signature? The computer has been a great productivity-enhancing tool, but a foil-stamped signature and an Avery® label is hardly a warm and fuzzy greeting of the season. We're not suggesting that you stop sending holiday cards or abandon common seasonal activities. Sometimes you have to do these things or you will be noticed by virtue of your absence.

Instead, expand your activities beyond the predictable. Add a personal note to your holiday cards. This takes time but people notice. We love it when we see people who remember that relationships are personal. It makes a huge difference when you personalize your correspondence.

Here are some examples of adding creativity to your standard networking and marketing:

- Create a calendar magnet highlighting the different restaurants where kids eat free on certain days of the week. Then package it in an envelope with a creative and funny message.

- Show up to your client's office with a batch of fresh cookies and a pint of milk with balloons to congratulate them on their new home. Not only will it surprise and delight them, but also their office-mates will share in the excitement. This is a great way to get the whole office talking about you.

- Track the interests, hobbies, favorite restaurants, and other pertinent information in your Sphere of Influence. You can then segment your database and start sending relevant information to your contacts instead of the throwaways that are common in the industry. For instance, if you have golfers in your database and you see a great article about Tiger Woods in the paper, you can cut that article out, copy it, and send it to them with a personal note telling them that the article made you think of them.

Hosting memorable events is a way to have personal interaction with clients, potential clients, referral sources, and other key influencers. Give people a compelling reason to attend. Here are a few examples:

- Hosting a grand opening at your new offices
- Introducing your new CEO/Broker to clients, partners, and the media
- Featuring your town's hot new chef at a private party held at one of your listings
- Collecting back-to-school supplies for low-income children in your community
- Having a well-known and slightly controversial industry expert as a guest speaker
- Hosting a fall festival at a rented orchard with activities such as face painting, hay rides, and pumpkin carving. Better yet is to make it a benefit for a local children's charity by encouraging all to bring a new, unwrapped toy.

There are many types of events that can be effective ways to network with your target market, including easy-to-coordinate informal and inexpensive options.

Small Gatherings: When it comes to networking, bigger events are not necessarily better. Gathering with small groups of strategically selected people is a good use of your networking time and dollars. If, for example, you and five colleagues each bring one new person to a lunch, you meet and spend time with five new people — certainly a networking success. A complementary business (such as a lender or a home inspector) might also co-host an event with you for both their clients and yours. While your clients get to meet one another, the two businesses also get to meet potential clients.

Sporting Events: One of the most traditional and effective ways to bond with other people is through sports. On any given day there is a business, charitable, or social golf tournament where new contacts are made, friendships are strengthened, and deals are struck. The fact that it is a scenic, quiet game played over the course of several hours lends itself to conversation. Skilled golfers truly love the game, and that in itself can lead to a strong connection between players as they discuss courses, equipment, and handicaps. Most golfers today are men, and in the business world that puts them at an advantage. The lesson here for women? Pick up those clubs! It could be one of the best networking moves you ever make.

Some agents may also have tickets or luxury box suites for their local university or professional sports teams. If used correctly, these can have great impact. If you have access to these types of tickets, think long and hard about how you use them. Attending a game with someone is much more beneficial to your relationship than giving them the tickets as a gift. And if you are asked to attend a sporting event with a business colleague, think twice before turning it down, even if you don't enjoy the sport. You will be sharing in the experience with your host, which is valuable. Sporting events generally last about three hours, and much of that time is spent socializing. You may even discover you like a sport once you have been exposed to it a few times.

Piggy Back Events: This strategy allows you to leverage other events to ensure attendance at your event, "piggy backing" one onto the other. For example, if there is a cocktail party honoring a retiring community leader from 6:00 – 8:00 p.m., this is a great opportunity to plan a dinner at a nearby restaurant starting at 8:30 p.m. Call ahead of time and invite some guests who you know will be at the main event. That way they will know in advance that they will be out later. Also, they will inevitably tell others that they were invited to dinner with you, which is good for your brand awareness and reputation. Save a couple of seats for people you meet at the event. The piggy back strategy also works well when attending industry conferences and trade shows. Check the schedule in advance to see if there is a night when there is no official event planned, and coordinate a small dinner with selected attendees. Or, reserve a suite in the hotel in which the conference is being held, and host a gathering prior to a speaker dinner.

You can make an event memorable by including a unique or unexpected twist, a thoughtful and strategic guest list, or a truly personal touch. Consider the imaginative networking ideas below.

Dave frequently entertains clients at dinner and has developed a trademark dining style. He asks the waitperson to serve two of the restaurant's signature desserts as the appetizer — a fun, surprising touch that is appreciated by his guests.

Each summer, Ellen invites her clients, prospects, and key referral sources to bring their spouses and children to a private Sunday afternoon screening of a new animated feature film. She has special wrist bands for everyone so that the popcorn, candy, and soft drinks are added to her tab.

Carlos and Lorenzo are business partners and sponsors of their local theatre group. They host a customer event that is a dress rehearsal for an upcoming performance, followed by a cocktail party with the actors and director.

Maria invites her contacts to be part of her team walking her local Juvenile Diabetes Research Foundation 5K. She even creates a team t-shirt featuring the logos of all participating companies.

Utilizing your network to help others find work

People embrace active networking the most when they are looking for a job. There's nothing like a pink slip to spur someone to crack open their contact database, schedule meetings with colleagues, and attend industry events. This isn't surprising since networking is by far the best way to find a next job. It also works for people exploring new career options. You can help others who have been laid off by utilizing your network. Consider this next scenario when you hear of someone that is looking for work.

Chad was approached by a former client. John had been very successful at his past job, but was looking to do something new and exciting although he was not sure what he wanted to do. John and Chad had lunch and talked about John's strengths and what he liked to do. They also talked about real estate and what a career in the business looked like. Can you guess where this story goes? John got his real estate license and became one of Chad's top agents.

The bottom line is this: utilize your network and be willing to help people in any way that you can. Open yourself up to the opportunity to help people by connecting them with others and you may create a relationship that will change your life — and theirs!

Some Networking Ideas for Women

Women abound in the real estate business. They may find networking challenging because of the "good ole boy" mentality that still exists in some places. This can be an intimidating and isolating situation, and is more common than you might think despite the approximately 72 million working female Americans.[8]

We touch on a few women's issues here and also suggest you read *Some Assembly Required: A Networking Guide for Women,* written by Thom Singer with Marny Lifshen, (New Year Publishing, 2008).

---

[8] Source – United States Department of Labor, 2008

Building successful relationships is often different for men than for women. Sadly, women are sometimes ostracized, patronized, or simply overlooked by male colleagues. Some men may be overtly rude, confrontational, or sexist, while others may just be uncomfortable having a woman in their work environment and avoid interaction altogether. Whether dealing with male brokers, managers, employees, or peers, even today, being a strong woman in real estate can be tough.

How can you overcome this challenge?

Use your skills and abilities. Instead of trying to blend in with the guys, leverage your innate differences. Add the personal touch by asking your male peers about their families, their vacations, and their hobbies. Use your social skills to shine at networking events. Utilize follow-up tools. Follow your intuition to pursue positive people and opportunities.

Relate to your male colleagues. Connect with your male co-workers on both a professional and personal level. You will have things in common; you just have to find them. Even if you do not share their interests, if you can engage in conversation with them you will find it easier to network. Take the time to learn a little about a few of these areas, and be prepared to join in the guy talk. Also, talk with them about your sellers and buyers, your industry, and your company. These topics bridge the gender gap and can help you build rapport.

Reach out to other women in your situation. There is great power in uniting with your sisters; no one knows better what you are going through. Not every female colleague will be your friend simply because you share a gender, but you will find an ally here and there. Women tend to look out for one another. Don't forget to establish a meaningful relationship first.

Identify supportive male colleagues and focus on them. Most men are perfectly comfortable working with women. Instead of worrying about how to handle the occasional jerk, focus on building relationships with the good guys. It'll be obvious who they are. They will include you in conversations, decisions, and opportunities, and will be assets in your network. Additionally, some men develop a fatherly relationship with younger female colleagues, serving as valuable mentors and champions. These men can be a great resource, as they can be well connected and will happily open their networks. So, while you will encounter some men who are not evolved, don't let those guys sour you on networking.

As with all networking, it will take time for these techniques to pay off, but you can succeed even in a challenging environment.

Networking with an open mind

One of the best things about networking is the wide variety of people you will meet. You'll encounter them in diverse venues, and build relationships in different ways. Even if it's more comfortable to spend time with people just like yourself, the contacts that can help you achieve your networking goals may be, in fact, quite varied. Meeting these kinds of people will push you out of your comfort zone and make you a stronger networker and a stronger agent.

Differences can occur between generations just as easily as they occur between genders and cultures. Keep an open mind and be respectful while learning to connect with different types of people. Focus on the commonalities that will lead toward your desired results.

It is easy to see the differences as The Continental Divide. In fact, some of the most successful and enjoyable relationships form between people who are from vastly different backgrounds or who are in different stages of life. Consider networking as an opportunity to meet and learn from a wide range of interesting people.

FAQ

Must I learn to golf? It can't hurt. In the real estate industry, golf can be an important tool for client entertaining, especially if you sell golf course properties. Similarly, if you're in an area where client entertaining happens to center around fly fishing, consider that. Many business people have learned to play golf and enjoy the sport. However, if you are not good at the game, or do not want to learn, then just accept the fact that this is not going to be your arena to network.

What do I do if I am just not creative? First, stop telling yourself that. Everyone can be creative; take time away to free-form think and write. Look at other industries to see what they are doing and use that as a jumping-off point. Look at the top people in your local board of realtors and see how they differentiate themselves. If all else fails, ask someone to help you.

Are there any don'ts in client entertaining? Oh yes. It would be wise to steer clear of any religious activities or political functions if you are not sure about your client's views on these subjects, as it may end up turning them off. Also, be careful when drinking in the presence of your clients. It's always best to let them order first.

7

YOUR TOOLBOX:

TRICKS OF THE TRADE

Now that you have defined your networking goals and developed your strategy, it's time to put your plan into action. There are several effective tools that will ease you into active networking, and help you be more effective.

Tools for networking events

Business Cards: Your business card is your single most important tool. Real estate agents need to carry cards with them at all times. You never know when you'll meet someone new or run into an old acquaintance, and your card is an easy and unobtrusive way to be sure they take away something useful from your conversation. Networking opportunities happen in all sorts of environments, from business functions to the dentist's office or the grocery store, and from dinner parties to your child's soccer games.

In addition to containing your pertinent contact information, your business card is an opportunity to make a positive impression. It helps someone develop an interest in your company or services, and it sets you apart. While it is increasingly common for professionals to simply transfer contact information from business cards to PDAs or databases, your card still gives you the chance to reinforce your personal brand.

Here are some business card pointers:

Make sure your business card looks professional. Business cards are a part of your image. If you don't have a lot of experience in marketing or graphic design, hire a designer to create your card. This is an investment that will pay off. Do not be the agent with the cheap looking and flimsy white paper card.

If you do not believe your broker has invested properly in your business cards, you probably do not believe they are up to speed on other things either. Be proactive and discuss improving the image of your company or change brokerages if you think that the tools provided are substandard. You are being judged by every aspect of your business, including the quality and look of your business cards.

Make sure your contact information is up-to-date. You do not want to be scratching off old data or hand writing in a new phone number; it brands you as disorganized and unprofessional. Don't forget to include your email address and website.

Use color on your card. Years ago, having color on your business card was cost prohibitive. Today color is inexpensive and will help to make you and your card memorable. Many professionals still subscribe to the idea of having a classic business card of raised black ink on a white or beige card. If you do this, just know that you will not stand out. Finally, leave the reverse side of the card a light color or white so people can jot notes on it if they wish.

Have your updated picture on the card. Having a photo on a business card has become common in the real estate business because it works! It makes you memorable. When you are out at conventions or networking it allows people to put a face with the name. Make sure that your photograph is a professional one. A good picture is worth the investment and can be used again and again in your other marketing materials.

Be brief. Your business card is not your resume or a marketing brochure. Very often agents try to list every possible service they can offer on their cards. If too much information is included people will be less likely to read it. If the card is cluttered or contains gimmicky slogans or other jargon, it will appear unprofessional. If you do a good job of making a connection, then your name, company, and basic contact information should be enough to trigger a reminder.

Use the standard size and shape. As memorable as unusually cut and sized business cards are, it's best to stick with the standard as it may not easily fit in a pocket or purse. Additionally, it may not fit within the recipient's filing system and into their database.

Nametags: The purpose of wearing a nametag at an event is to facilitate conversations. If someone's nametag reads "Bill Smith – Exxon," you can approach them with "Hi, Bill, I have a friend that works for Exxon." If the company is lesser known you might say "Mary, I haven't heard of The Hill Group. What does your company do?" Many times people choose not to wear nametags (or, frighteningly, the organization hosting the event does not provide them) or the text is too small for the average person to read. This is a missed opportunity since people are more likely to approach someone new when his or her name is in plain view.

Some real estate professionals go even further and have a permanent plastic or metal nametag created and wear it at all times. This is a personal choice based on your company's culture.

Keep these tips in mind for the next time you write your own nametag at an event:

1. Make it legible. Print clearly and neatly.

2. Make it informative. Include your first and last name, with your company's name underneath. Be sure to use the version of your company's name that most people will recognize, avoiding internal nicknames or initials if they are not widely known. If you work for Century 21, people in the business

will know what C21 is, but those outside the industry might not. Abbreviating Coldwell Banker to "CB" or Keller Williams to KW means nothing to the masses. Consider your audience.

3. Make it visible. Wear your nametag where it can be easily seen. If you are wearing a jacket or coat, place it there. The best spot is on your right shoulder, as when you are shaking hands with someone it is a natural line of sight along the outstretched arm to the shoulder.

A Personal Tag Line: It is not uncommon to stumble when answering simple questions like "What do you do?" or "What does your company do?" While you certainly know the answer, verbalizing it in a clear, compelling way is a bigger challenge. Instead of just telling someone that you sell homes, think of an answer that is more compelling.

Consider these very different answers to the standard question "So, what do you do?"

Good: I work for a real estate company.

Better: I'm a realtor.

Best: I assist people in making what is usually the single biggest purchase of their lives — their home.

Good: I am in real estate.

Better: I work in residential real estate.

Best: I am a residential real estate professional who works with people who are buying and selling homes.

Rehearse your personal tag line until it flows naturally. Try writing different versions down on paper to help you refine your ideas. Practice your tag line with your spouse, friends, or co-workers and get their feedback. There can be a fine line between interesting and cheesy, and you'll need someone you trust to tell you if you've crossed it. Once you have refined your tag line, practice, practice, practice. Taking the time to perfect your presentation will make you more comfortable and confident when it comes time to say it to someone you don't actually know. Your personal tag line is a work in progress so amend it as necessary. Your goal is to deliver relevant information while capturing the interest of a new contact.

Keeping yourself in the know

The newspaper and Internet: If you are to be a successful networker, you must be able to participate actively and intelligently in conversations. Whether you are mingling at an event or sitting at a conference table, you should be able to converse about current events. To do this, you must keep current on the news.

Imagine this: While attending a conference, you take a seat at the luncheon table and find all your peers talking about the acquisition of a major industry player. Since you know nothing about this, you are unable to participate in the discussion. This scenario is played out in networking events each day. When you are not up-to-date about what is happening in the world, you are at a disadvantage.

With so much information available on the Internet, there is no excuse for not keeping up with important news. Regardless of whether you prefer the online or paper version, read the local news each day, scanning each section and reading the business section completely. Keep up with what is happening in local politics, especially as it pertains to zoning, education, and everything real estate!

If your community has a weekly business journal, add that to your required reading list. Also, it's smart to read national newsweeklies such as *Time, US News & World Report, or Newsweek*. Finally, read the publications that are specific to the real estate industry. A balance of media is best, and will help insure that you can connect through conversation while networking.

It can also be a distinct advantage to keep up with the major sports stories. Men often outnumber women at networking functions, and sports are a common topic of discussion. You don't have to be an expert, or even really like sports (although it certainly helps if you do); you just need to know what people are talking about.

Beyond sports, it is also good to keep up with pop culture. While you might not have any interest in whom Madonna is dating, you would be surprised how often television, music, and celebrities come up in casual conversation. Glancing over the covers of the supermarket tabloids will give you just enough knowledge to get by.

Finding the time to be well read is a challenge. Like anything, if you make reading a regular part of your schedule, it will become easier. If you fall behind reading periodicals, throw away back copies and start fresh with the most current issues. Devoting 30 minutes each day to reading should be enough to stay current.

Follow-up tools

Letters and emails: One of the best ways to follow up with someone is to send them a short, handwritten note. In today's electronic world, a handwritten note has become rare, and thus more memorable. Realtors should send out a minimum of four handwritten notes a day. They take little time once you are in the habit, and they will make you stand out. Here is an example:

Dear Allen,

It was a pleasure to talk with you at the Chamber dinner last night. I enjoyed learning about your company and wish you much continued success. Please let me know if I can ever be of any assistance for you in buying or selling real estate. I hope to see you again soon. Let me know if I can help you in your business!

Best wishes,
Liam Cook

Consider sending correspondence to set you apart. Branding is a continual process so it's nice to have personal notes that have your logo and tagline, if you've developed one. When you read an article that features or mentions a person you know well, clip it and send it to that person with a note. He or she will be flattered that you took the time to pass it on. This strategy also works if you read an article that a member of your network would find interesting. For example, if you read a story about a traveling art exhibit coming to your city and know someone who loves the artist, clip and send them the article. If the piece is online, email them the link with a note saying, "Thought you would enjoy this article." Do not forward mass email links to your entire database, though; that does not show any personal thought and is instead annoying.

Following up with an email is the quickest way to reach out after meeting someone, although you run the risk of your message getting lost in spam filters or amongst the many emails that person receives each day. While some people read email immediately, others have hundreds of messages hanging out in their inbox so it could be weeks before they read yours. Remember that how you use email is not necessarily the same for everyone. Do not assume your email is being read. And, if you're among those who do not spell-check their email, you could do some serious damage to your brand.

When you do use email, keep it brief. Remind the person about where and when you met, and suggest or confirm next steps. Do not include several screens of information or attach a brochure. Attachments will often land your correspondence in the spam folder. An email after you have just met someone is not a solicitation for business, but rather a vehicle for you to convey how much you enjoyed your initial meeting.

Home Buyers' or Sellers' Guides and Newsletters: When someone you have met indicates that they are interested in learning more about your company, sending them a follow-up letter and enclosing a guide is a great next step. These guides can provide information on your company's marketing plan, including lengthy details that aren't appropriate for a follow-up letter or email. A well-made home sellers' guide is a good tool for the educational phase of networking.

Newsletters are another great way to demonstrate your expertise. However, so many companies now have some form of newsletter that you need to find a compelling reason for people to read yours. Make sure the information is relevant. It should include timely, helpful information in a well-designed format, and some kind of hook. By law, you must give people the option of being removed from your distribution list. Make sure to ask people permission to "add them to your VIP list." Sending a lot of impersonal email is a great way to turn someone off so be sure to encourage them to opt in.

One real estate brokerage we know created a monthly newsletter for its clients and friends. In addition to its standard content about the market, it includes a trivia quiz of little-known facts about Austin. Readers can email or call in their answer, and on the 15th of each month there is a drawing for a $100 gift certificate to a local restaurant. This quiz generates dozens of correct responses each month and in the following month's newsletter the winner and answer are called out. This is a great way to connect with your community.

Websites, Blogs, and a Presence on Social Networking Websites: These days, when we meet someone new or run into a former colleague, we go back to the office, fire up our browser and look them up. Be confident that others are doing the same thing when they meet you. Websites are a good source of information on an agent and his or her business. Well-designed, professionally written websites can provide a consumer with a solid overview of your company's mission, homes that you have for sale, and a search engine component that allows people to sign up to work with your company. Your website can play a big part in a person deciding if they want to pursue a relationship further.

Many agents are also now designing their own personal blogs and social networking pages. Savvy agents use blogs to promote their personal brands and establish themselves as thought leaders.

Blogging involves a time commitment to regularly create relevant posts that provide value and encourage readers to keep coming back. If you are successful, your blog becomes part of your networking efforts and your personal brand. However, do not start a blog if you do not plan on updating it regularly, as an abandoned blog can send a message that you do not follow through on your projects.

If you are going to maintain a business website, blog, or social networking page, the content must be professional in nature. According to a study done by the National Association of Realtors, 86% of buyers and sellers are now starting their searches online. Your presence or absence on the Internet can play a huge factor in your success as an agent. Use every tool you can to capture your audience. And remember, there's a business-appropriate way to utilize personal blogs or profiles on social networking sites. Be careful what content you include.

Resumes and Biographies: While most realtors have brochures and websites to describe their homes for sale and marketing plan, they often forget to add the human element. Resumes and bios are tools that focus on you.

Bios are a general summary of your experience and expertise, and are usually in paragraph form. Rather than listing the names of your employers and dates of your employment, bios emphasize the highlights of your career and your special skills. Both your resume and your bio should include your membership and leadership roles in professional and community organizations.

It's okay to include your family, interests, and hobbies in your biographical information. However, you should avoid being too personal or including things that could put people off. Religion is one of those areas. It is a personal decision to discuss such matters, but be conscious of not looking intolerant of other belief systems. You want your business image to be respectful of all people who come into contact with you.

Realizing that you have tools at your disposal that can make you stand out from the competition is just the first step. Take these ideas and implement them; create your own tool kit. A well-prepared and successful networking agent will always be ready when an opportunity presents itself.

Your Networking Tool Kit should include:

- Accurate, memorable, and professional business cards
- A clear, original, and well-rehearsed personal tag line
- Well-written follow-up letters and emails
- Appropriate, updated, and strategic websites, blogs, and social networking pages
- An updated and focused resume and biography

FAQ

What is the most appropriate time to give someone my business card and to ask for theirs? There is not a single most appropriate time to exchange business cards when meeting someone new, but it is often most comfortable when you are first introduced or after a brief introductory conversation. You can also exchange cards when you are parting ways, saying, "It was great to meet you. Here's my card; do you have one? I would love to keep in touch."

Where can I find a guide for writing a good resume and bio? We suggest looking at the resumes and bios of agents you admire and then using those as a rough guide. Obviously you cannot copy them word-for-word, but you can follow the format and tone to weave a powerful story about you and your experience. Including some fun personal info about your interests and hobbies can be a great way to connect with people.

What should I consider before writing a blog? Writing a blog is a big commitment of time and brain power. You must be ready to post new content three to five times a week. Blog readers always want something new, and a blog that has not been updated becomes stale very quickly. Also, consider the topics that you will cover. A good pre-blogging strategy is to make a list of 50 things you will blog about. If this comes easily to you then you may be ready to blog.

A blog must have a focus and a theme, and while you can go off-topic on occasion, your readers will come back regularly because they care about your message. Having a blog can help position you as an expert, but that won't happen overnight. It can take years to find your audience, so be patient and tenacious.

How much money will it cost me to invest in a good website? There are as many options for building a website as there are types of coffee drinks at Starbucks. You can do it yourself, you can hire a company, you can purchase pre-designed templates that you will just add your logos and photos to, or you can do some combination of the above. If you are inclined to create your own, the major cost will be your time and energy away from selling. Hiring a company to do it for you can cost as little as $500 up to $25,000. Purchasing a pre-designed web template usually will run in the $3,000-$5,000 range. Research your options well and ask others in your network for their experience and their input.

8

MENTORS, PEER GROUPS,
AND COACHES

The Road of Life is a bumpy one, filled with both obstacles and opportunities. What did you know about real estate before you got into it? Not as much as you know now, right? When you enter any business, there is a lot to learn. If you are fortunate enough to instinctively know which way to turn at every fork in the road, and if everyone you meet provides you with excellent advice, then you are very lucky.

For the rest of us, it is helpful to have some special people whom we can turn to for guidance and, on occasion, tough love. Keeping an open mind and being aware that you can learn from others is a key factor to your success. It is especially valuable to discover these people early in your career. Whether they are mentors, peer groups, or coaches, these people can be an important part of your long-term success, and can help you minimize many of the hazards that will come along with building your real estate career. As in all networking relationships, these are give-and-take partnerships. Be sure that you offer to help as often as you ask for it.

What is a mentor?

A mentor is a wise and trusted teacher or counselor. Anyone with more experience than you in a particular area can be your mentor. He or she can be older or younger, as long as they have lived the experiences that will allow them to provide informed advice. The relationship can be a formal one where you have scheduled meetings with specific agendas, or it can be so informal that neither of you even realizes that the person is even mentoring you.

Ideally, you should have multiple mentors that bring a different perspective or expertise so that no matter what your issue, you have someone with relevant experience to turn to. Your mentors do not even need to be in the real estate business.

Saul is a successful agent who gets much of his mentoring from his older brother, a technology sales professional. While the nature of the business challenges can be very different, the underlying sales skills are often the same. Saul and his brother often discuss how to better establish their professional brand in their respective industries.

One of Chad's mentors is leadership guru and bestselling author John Maxwell. Chad had read his books and for years John had been a virtual mentor via his writing. Over time they came to know each other personally and now John has become a formal mentor whom Chad speaks with a number of times a year. While John is not in real estate, his leadership expertise has been incredibly valuable in helping Chad construct his career.

A mentor is usually someone to whom you have direct access, although often people are inspired by virtual mentors. Oprah may be a role model for thousands upon thousands of women, but she is only a true mentor to a few. Your mentor is someone whom you regularly turn to for advice, someone who has taken a visible interest in assisting you along the path of your career. In fact, you may already have a mentor and not even realize it. Think back to the last time you had a difficult problem with a transaction. Or the last time you were considering letting go of an agent or an employee. Whose advice did you seek?

Some real estate firms offer agents formal mentoring programs. Agents are assigned to work with a team leader that will help them in any part of their business where they may be struggling. Each senior manager or executive will make themselves available to the agents to help them through the ins and outs of their sales and they will help teach how to hold a successful open house and teach them to write a business plan.

> **"Economic advantages may be created by people who surround themselves with the advice, counsel and personal cooperation of a group of people who are willing to lend them wholehearted aid in a spirit of perfect harmony. This form of cooperative alliance has been the basis of nearly every great fortune. Your understanding of this great truth may definitely determine your financial status."[9]**

---

[9] Napoleon Hill, *Think and Grow Rich,* pg 195, Copyright 2003 Penguin Books

A mentor does not have to come from inside your own company though or, as mentioned previously, even the industry. Very often people forget about the power of having mutually beneficial relationships with a wide variety of people, which includes competitors sometimes. In many cases it is helpful to have an outsider bring a fresh, unbiased perspective. This can be especially useful if you are dealing with sensitive client issues or office politics. While you want to take special care not to share sensitive information with competitors, a real friend in another company can give you an astute sense of perspective about your industry.

Consider Miyuki, who is trying to decide whether to remain on a residential real estate sales team or return to working with a builder. There are many factors to consider, including how her decision will impact her financial and professional future and her personal life. Other agents who have faced similar career crossroads will be the best source of relevant advice for Miyuki.

Regardless of where you find mentors, having them can help you stay focused on your career goals. They help you navigate rough stretches because they have been there before. A good mentor is someone that looks upon your problems as minor pitfalls, while helping you make the most of new opportunities — and perhaps take chances you might otherwise pass up. Try to find a mentor who is several steps ahead of you in their career, as he or she will most be able to help you achieve success.

Finding a mentor

If you want a structured mentoring relationship then you need to give some advance thought to what such an arrangement involves, and you may need to consider hiring a coach, which is covered toward the end of this chapter. You may also have some concerns about selecting the right person, especially if you do not already have someone in mind.

Start by identifying the issues you feel you need a mentor to help you tackle. Then, determine the characteristics that your ideal mentor will have:

1. Should they have a specific type of business or industry experience?

2. How old do you think this person should be?

3. What do you expect them to provide for you?

4. Is their physical location an issue?

5. How often will you plan to meet?

Women sometimes face gender-specific challenges in the real estate business so they may prefer to seek out female mentors. While men can certainly be valuable mentors to female professionals, there are some issues to which they may not relate, and therefore may be unable to provide relevant guidance. As you create your "ideal mentor" list, ask yourself if gender is a factor.

Brainstorm for a list of people who meet your requirements. This can be difficult, so take your time and try to include both people you know personally and those you know by reputation. You may also need to reach out to your network to ask other people to make recommendations.

Then, take the plunge and ask. If you do not know them personally, a good strategy is to have someone who does find out if that person would be receptive to a mentoring role. If the other person understands mentoring and is willing to discuss the idea with you, call to arrange an initial meeting. Be honest about how you see the relationship developing and the time commitment involved. Having specific objectives and accountability will help you stay focused on the goals of the relationship. You will also want to mutually agree upon strict confidentiality, because both of you will want to be at ease sharing personal and business information. For this reason it is also critical that there is good chemistry between you.

Be prepared to provide your new mentor with a summary of the topics that are on your mind, though these will change over time. Agree to a set period of time for the formal mentoring to take place (perhaps one year) and schedule meetings every other month. This will enable you to get to know one another; at the end of that time you can decide whether to continue in a structured relationship or move to an informal basis. If you do a good job of building a mutually beneficial relationship, there will be little need to discuss the ongoing relationship, as it will evolve naturally. Be sure to take the time to ask your mentor how you can help them.

Even if you are new to real estate, it might surprise you to realize that you, too, can be a mentor. Moreover, you should be a mentor. You do not need to have a 25-year career in real estate to be a valuable advisor to others. As you advance in your career and achieve higher levels of success, you can help others who are coming along behind you. As your path was most likely made easier by those who mentored you, you should take the time to guide others. It can be very rewarding, and it's not as time-consuming as you might think. New agents are always looking for guidance, and helping and sharing your experiences with others will help you both mentally and spiritually. It feels good to come to the aid of people in need.

Additionally, you have a wide variety of life experiences outside of your real estate career that can bring value to others, even those who are more seasoned in the business. Making yourself available could provide another person with just what they need to overcome their own obstacles.

As a mentor, you will have the ability to impact someone's life in many ways. Sharing your mistakes can help them avoid tripping up. Your positive examples and insight can assist them in making smart choices. Additionally, you can open up your network and introduce them to others who can present them with opportunities. This can also benefit you directly because as your protégé advances in his or her career and expands their own network, they will be in a position to help you. Sharing your experiences and advice will not only make you feel good, but in time it will also allow you to grow and learn.

What is a coach?

The difference between a coach and a mentor is that your coach is a paid advisor. There are several other differences between a coach and a mentor, but that is the main difference. There are many different levels of coaching and they range from as little as $50 a month to as much as $5,000 a month. It just depends on what level you are looking to go to and the frequency that you feel you need to speak with your coach.

A typical arrangement is to have two 30-minute calls a month. Additionally, there will be a lot of up-front work done by both you and your coach, things such as gathering your sales numbers, your marketing plan, your future goals, and the systems that you use to track all of your activities. Your coach will take this information and use it to develop a plan to help you move to the next level in your business. Also, the up-front observations will help your coach determine where you should focus your energy. On the calls, your coach will usually have very specific objectives to cover with you. There will usually be a set progression of what you are going to go over, and most of the time that will start with business planning. However, the call's content may be taken over by your current issues and challenges. There will also be some accountability to tasks that you and your coach both agree upon. You may talk about current prospecting efforts, marketing, or a variety of other important aspects of your business.

Your coach will hold you accountable. Let them be tough with you. You want someone that will hold you to the highest standards. Find a coach who specializes in real estate. There are many out there who are familiar with the idiosyncrasies of your day-to-day business.

One of the great things about coaches is that they deal with many different agents in many different markets and are thus in a position to share best practices. A good coach will handle 15-50 clients at a time. They will be able to give you real-time solutions that others have utilized to make things happen in their business. These coaches can also help you build your nationwide network. People that use the same coach often get to know each other and, in return, you may receive referrals and other opportunities from these other agents.

At some point you will outgrow your coach. Similar to releasing a listing because you have done everything you can with it marketing wise, you will get to a point where you have fully utilized your coach. Keep that in mind and make sure that you always end the relationship with the utmost respect and thankfulness. Burning bridges is never a good idea and an even worse thing to do with someone that has helped to change your life and your business.

Group coaching and webinars

Group coaching and webinars are another way to help expand your knowledge and your network. Group coaching is usually done on a specific topic and involves a coach giving a presentation for 30 minutes about how to improve in that area. Group coaching is a cost-effective and efficient way to mine ideas from people that have tons of real estate knowledge.

Webinars are another way to learn with other agents. Again, these are on a specific focus such as short sales, prospecting for sale by owners or business planning. You may be able to receive a list of the agents on the calls or webinars to expand your nationwide agent network.

What is a peer group?

In a nutshell, a peer group is made up of people at similar places in their careers that act as a personal advisory board for one another. Peer groups can be an important part of your network, as they provide you with a trusted group of colleagues that you can turn to for advice, resources, and support. Many agents use this model to share best practices. Ideally, peer groups provide an open and safe environment in which to test business ideas, discuss challenges and opportunities, and to gain honest feedback.

As with mentors, peer groups can be informal, occasional gatherings of select people, or a more formal organization with dues, bylaws, and specific membership requirements. In some cities, the local chamber of commerce organizes formal peer groups for business owners to meet other like-minded business owners. The Entrepreneurs' Organization, The Alternative Board, and the Women's Global Business Alliance also do this for their members.

Barbie is an agent with big goals. She is heavily investing in local radio and television advertising and has joined a peer group of agents around the country that focuses on what works, and does not work, with regard to how their ads are structured. They do conference calls a few times a year to share how they are running things and how each agent is growing and expanding his or her opportunity. It is an incredible way to learn and a great way again to expand your national network for great referrals.

Organizing your own peer group

Finding the right people to be a part of a peer group is similar to finding a mentor. While some people may be obvious, it's important to include those who are not already your close friends. Forming a group of your buddies does not give you any objectivity. Start by identifying two or three people you already know who are committed to growing their network and advancing their career. Pick agents that are dedicated to the same values and ideals that you are, but may run a different type of business or work in a different niche than you. You may want to include people who are outside of your industry or profession, as you will learn most by having a diversity of skills and experiences in your group.

Then, build the group by having each member look at his or her own contact lists and adding one or two more. Limit this to between five and ten people; peer groups function best in smaller numbers. This allows for some attrition while keeping it small enough for everyone to get to know one another and actively participate in meetings. While it's not crucial to keep the group's existence a secret, it is preferable because it prevents others from asking to join. Once the group begins meeting it's difficult to add people because of all the time that has been invested early on, and the trust and chemistry that already have been built amongst the participants.

Be sure to set the ground rules for your peer group early. Decide how often you should meet (at least monthly), and ask all members to make the commitment. If someone's work schedule is irregular and does not allow them to make most meetings, find someone else. As with a mentor relationship, confidentiality is a must. Discuss this at your first meeting, and get buy-in on the rules and structure of your peer group.

Make sure that everyone gets a chance to talk about themselves during the first few meetings; peer groups are not a place for people to stay on the sidelines and observe. In the future, each member can have the focus of a meeting to discuss his or her issues. While you can meet with members of your peer group one-on-one, the group dynamic can be very beneficial when you are wrestling with a problem or analyzing the pros and cons of an opportunity. An idea or opinion from one member of your peer group might spawn an idea from another member, leading to a creative and productive session.

For the group to succeed, everyone must make attendance and active participation a priority. Keep in mind that even with a successful set of people who develop close relationships, the group will eventually play itself out. That's just fine; it has served its purpose and chances are, the friendships developed within the peer group will last.

Having a group of advisors to bounce ideas off of is invaluable. When you start sharing your ideas, the synergy of other people's creativity can spark your mind and help you to formulate a more powerful concept.

Nothing great has ever been achieved by a single person. If you look at the most successful accomplishments throughout history you will find that there were teams of people supporting the effort. The Lone Ranger is a myth. You need mentors, peer groups, and coaches if you want to reach the top.

FAQ

My mentor is not what I'd envisioned; how do I make this work? Make sure you have clearly defined and articulated the kind of assistance you would like from your mentor; there simply may be a communication problem. Try beginning your next meeting by reiterating your goals, and determining if you can meet them together. If not, it should be clear to both of you that the mentoring has not worked out in this particular pairing. That's okay. Move on.

Where should our peer group meet? Meeting at one of the member's offices is a good idea, especially if it's an agent that has a good setup that you can learn from. If your peer group is a local network of different professions, a coffee shop or a restaurant can work well. Regardless of where you meet, choose a location that is conveniently located for all participants.

I like some people in my peer group more than others; how do I handle that? Learn to find good in all people. It is natural that you click with some members more than others. It is important, however, that you behave professionally with everyone, and that you are inclusive and supportive. Even if your relationships with a few members become more important and mutually beneficial, work hard to avoid cliques developing within your peer group.

My mentor intimidates me; she is such a mover and shaker that I can't relate to her at all. How do I get her to take it down a notch for me? First, thank your lucky stars that someone so influential has agreed to be your mentor. Next, pat yourself on the back since you are clearly worthy of such a relationship. Try to take advantage of the counsel and connections your mentor brings, even if it means stretching beyond your comfort zone. If the advice you get and the opportunities you are presented are beyond your current capabilities, encourage your mentor to give you more attainable goals, being as specific as possible and very, very thankful of their efforts.

9

NETWORKING ONLINE

Since the arrival of the Internet in our daily lives, people have communicated with others around the world using email, bulletin boards, chat rooms, social networking websites and other tools. While the term "networking" once only applied to initiating and cultivating relationships in person, the web has added an entirely new dimension. Today, a huge population of social and professional contacts is within reach via the computer. Many people have chosen to avoid this part of networking altogether because they do not understand its power or are overwhelmed by it. But online networking is not complicated and, if used correctly, can be an effective and enjoyable part of your experience. As a real estate agent whose career depends on contacts, this is a necessary part of your repertoire.

The electronic world of networking does not replace face-to-face networking, but it can help you cultivate existing and new relationships in ways that you could never have imagined just a few years ago.

Don't be fooled by the term "social networking" as it is for business. The word "social" differentiates it from "computer networking" (*i.e.,* your internal or external network of computers, servers, routers, etc. ... as opposed to a stand-alone computer). Many real estate professionals dismiss the trend of online networking as they mistakenly think it is just something you do with your friends.

What is online networking?

Online networking means different things to different people. The online networking practices of a 19-year-old college student are vastly different from those of a 40-year-old real estate agent. This book focuses on the needs of the real estate agent. Online networking only differs from face-to-face networking in that you may never actually meet or have spoken with the people in your network, but to create meaningful connections still takes a commitment. With online networking, you use the Internet's reach to facilitate the process. Many of the strategies used in traditional networking apply in cyberspace, but there are some different strategies and rules as well.

There is a tendency to view online tools as a magic bullet, especially if you're reticent to attend networking events and are, perhaps, an introvert. You can easily look at the number of online connections you have and feel confident that you are doing a good job of creating a network, when, in fact, this may not be the case. Think of online networking as just one of your strategies, one that provides flexibility and gives you access to a whole world of contacts, literally.

Types of online networking

There are many different tools that allow you to network online. While the social networking (a term used to describe a variety of Internet-based activities and communities) does not replace the importance of face-to-face networking, it is a powerful complement.

A social networking site is a website that maintains an online database of people and enables participants to search and contact other users. These sites have exploded onto the scene during the last several years, fast becoming more than a fad or a part of pop culture, but instead becoming a regular tool used by millions on a daily basis. These sites have evolved from something used mostly by teenagers and college students to something mass market. While the databases that these websites manage are enormous, most communication is one-on-one. As a member, you utilize the site to identify, learn about, and contact other members individually.

LinkedIn, Facebook, MySpace, Twitter, Plaxo, Friendster, Yammer, Ryze, and *Ecademy* offer people the chance to expand their contacts and build business relationships. MySpace is also used by professionals to create virtual brochures in an effort to reach others who share similar interests. *Facebook* and *LinkedIn* are the most common sites that are being used in this professional capacity and have thousands of professional groups focused on local, national, and international topics of interest. As a member of social networking sites, you can join and create customized online communities that meet your individual needs.

Sites such as *LinkedIn* focus exclusively on the needs of professionals looking to network with colleagues, sell their products and services, find new jobs, or recruit employees. Proper management of such contacts can lead to increased sales and opportunities, so these sites get a lot of attention. For you as a real estate agent, there is a great opportunity to connect with people you would not otherwise meet. Through a contact on *LinkedIn*, Vivienne met someone in the commercial real estate business. They set up a face-to-face meeting and figured out a way to refer each other and a great business relationship was formed. It can be that easy, but you have to make the effort and utilize the technology.

Posting a profile on these services is usually free, but many have levels of membership that offer advanced benefits for a nominal fee. The trick is getting to know the different options that exist and participating in the online social networking platform that best suits your needs. Be sure to create and maintain an accurate profile because this will help ensure that people who want to meet someone with your expertise or interests can find you.

One common mistake people make is to create a profile that contains little or no information. Make sure that the information you share helps people understand who you are. If you hide too much information, you will be seen as not really engaged. Take your time to explore the profiles of your friends, co-workers, competitors, and others to best understand what type of information you should expose.

Twitter is another tool that has become popular with many in the real estate business. It's often referred to as micro-blogging, as it is used similarly to a blog yet it has only 140 characters to get your point across. Some people think that *Twitter* is a waste of time and do not understand why anyone would care what they were doing at any given moment. However, for some, it is an important part of their communication and self-branding strategy. Across the US, many real estate professionals follow each other on *Twitter* and build referral relationships by sharing thoughts, ideas, best practices, etc.

By mutually following each other's "tweets" or messages, people can shorten the time it takes to get to know one another. There are geographically based "Tweet Ups" where people in a given city will meet at a local restaurant or other location to get to know other *Twitter* users face-to-face.

Be conscious of what you tweet, or post to any social media site as people are watching and judging you by your actions. There are countless stories of people losing deals or jobs because they tweeted or posted something inappropriate.

Benefits of online networking for realtors

The benefits of participating in an online networking
community can be many if the membership includes the
demographics of professionals with whom you wish to
connect. It can help you:

Manage contact information: Some online services, like
LinkedIn, can be used to efficiently manage your contacts,
while others, such as Plaxo, integrate with traditional
contact management systems. It's an easy way to regularly
review your connections and keep up with their current
career status. People change jobs often and it's easy to
lose touch when their email address and phone numbers
change. As a savvy agent, you always want to have up-
to-date information on your past clients and Sphere of
Influence. Likewise, if you have a profile on a social networking site then people will always be able to find you.

Find connections: These sites also make it simple for you
to see whom your contacts are connected to. Some users
keep their connections private, but often they are available for viewing. By regularly reviewing the lists of people
you're connected to, you can identify professionals you
might wish to do business with and who can make the
introduction. Additionally, if there is someone you are
looking to meet, you can trace the connection path back to

your network. You'll be surprised how often the one person who can make an important introduction is someone you regularly interact with.

Raise your profile: Online networking is an effective way to reach important influencers. Recruiters are not the only folks relying on the web to source qualified candidates; journalists search for subject matter experts and conference planners source topical speakers. More and more business professionals are going online to find vendors, partners, and consultants. Managing your online reputation, therefore, is an important part of your ongoing career plan and your personal brand.

Updating your status: Most sites give you the ability to post a short sentence about what you are working on at any given moment. Using this part of your page in a social networking community allows you to remind your contacts that you are an active part of their online network. Your update appears in an ongoing "stream" on their page, mixed in with status updates from others. Remember that out of sight is out of mind, so keeping your contacts up to date is important. However, there is a fine line between sharing information and overdoing it. Some people post too many updates and flood their contacts with too much information. This will annoy some people and they will delete you from their contact list. Find a balance.

Twitter, however, is the exception to this rule. *Twitter* is meant to be updated frequently. Some people have their *Twitter* stream to flow directly to their status update on *Facebook*. We do not recommend this as it is annoying to non-*Twitter* users on *Facebook*. The things you might say or the frequency you might comment is different in each environment. It is acceptable to tweet frequently and make random and obscure comments. Your *Facebook* connections may want more meaningful information in your status updates. While there are no rules, remember that you have an audience in each social networking community and they are not always the same.

Social networking is being utilized in more and more ways, impacting many segments of our society. It is changing, for example, the way that people contribute to charitable and community causes. Tapping into someone's online network is an efficient and effective way to raise awareness and funds, and many charities are developing strategies to do just that. But individuals, too, are using social networks to get involved, where they might not have known how to help in the past.

Quantity vs. quality

Some people view the quantity of connections as the most important element of online networking. These people invite hundreds (if not thousands) of people to join their networks without ever having met them. On *LinkedIn* these users are commonly referred to as LIONs, *LinkedIn* Open Networkers. They link to anyone and everyone, regardless of where they live, what they do, or if they have any real reason to be connected in the real world. We do not recommend this practice as it diminishes the power of your network. Keep in mind that the more time you spend with online networking, the more time you will find it takes to manage all of your digital contacts. There are no shortcuts to networking, even online.

If a virtual stranger sends you a link request, and you do not want to accept the connection, just ignore and archive the invitation. If you click the "I don't know them" option, *LinkedIn* will put them on a list that could suspend their account for trying to link to a stranger. While our opinion is that their action of linking to everyone is not the right thing to do, we are not the Networking Police. There is no need to punish them for having a different online networking philosophy.

Thom's rule of thumb is that he will not link to anyone whom he has not spent one hour with over coffee, breakfast, or happy hour engaged in conversation, or the digital equivalent. (The digital equivalent means that over time via email, phone, and online networking you can reach a similar level of comfort with someone that you would in a face-to-face meeting). His reasoning is that if you are going to refer or do business with someone, you want to know more about them than what you can learn from their *Facebook* page. You want to actually have a personal connection. To phone someone you don't know is cold-calling, not networking.

Since members of online communities are not pre-screened, you have no way of knowing the goals of people you might encounter. Just because someone has a profile on a social networking site does not mean they welcome everyone on the planet to contact them. Do not assume you have the right to reach out to them because you stumbled upon their profile online.

Staying safe online

An unfortunate reality of online networking is that having a digital connection to someone does not automatically make them reputable. It is difficult to know someone by only reading his or her profile or exchanging a few emails. Working in the same industry or having similar interests is not enough common ground for a strong and mutually beneficial business relationship. Communicating via email leaves a great deal open to interpretation, which can lead to misunderstanding or can even be dangerous.

Women especially need to be careful when establishing online connections, even ones that have been referred by a close friend or business associate. While it's no fun considering the dark underbelly of the web, there are people using it for all the wrong reasons. Keep your guard up. These are not the right forums for disclosing your home address or phone number. If you do decide to meet someone in person that you have met through online networking, make sure to do so in a public place and bring along a friend or co-worker. Better safe than sorry is the best motto when crossing from online connections to face-to-face connections.

We also recommend against announcing on your blog or in a social media community when you are away from home. While it is tempting to tell your friends about your great trip to Spain, you could also unwittingly be telling potential thieves that your home is unoccupied for two weeks. If you decide to post on your travels while travelling just be aware that others, beyond your friends, can see the information.

It is important that you do not ignore the possibilities that online social networking can bring to your career. You do not need to be active in every social media community out there but you should be aware about their existence and make informed decisions as to when to participate and when not to be involved. Making blanket decisions that these tools are frivolous or just for the younger crowd could be a costly mistake for you as you look toward the future of your real estate career.

FAQ

Should I post my picture on a social networking site? This is becoming increasingly common online; however, you should not post your photo if you are not comfortable with having it visible to anyone. While it makes you more identifiable and "real" to those that you are connected with, use caution about putting too much personal information online. Realtors generally have pictures on their business cards so most realtors will have them online, too. Alternatively, you can create an avatar, a cartoon-like image that represents you. This is a fun way to present yourself without the risks associated with photography.

Is online networking time-consuming? One of the downsides to online social networking is that it can be addictively time-consuming. You need to spend time, just as in face-to-face networking, sharing experiences and building the relationship. Spending time on these sites and sending messages to your contacts can be a huge time drain. Visit your social networking sites periodically so that you do not get lost in cyberspace.

Does joining an online community put me at greater risk for spam or viruses? Yes. But you have a spam filter and up-to-date antivirus software, right? One way to cut down on the amount of spam you receive is to post your email address in a comment on a blog or other site, as "goofy @ disneyland.com." This will prevent automated spammers from being able to identify your address and will cut down on your chances of ending up on spam lists. As for viruses, never download documents unless you trust the source.

How frequently do I need to participate in an online forum to benefit? This will vary from group to group. Nothing of value comes without some level of commitment, so you'll need to invest some time. Devote a few hours a week to social networking and you'll see a payoff. If you come to think that the community you are participating in is not worth the time, move on.

10

THE FINISHING TOUCHES: TURNING YOUR NETWORK INTO REAL BUSINESS

Some people work hard to build relationships with others, yet never ask them for help. Just as building strong business relationships is a learned skill, asking those in your network to help you is a learned skill. Most real estate agents have trouble when it comes right down to asking for referrals, claiming that they don't want to be pushy. Be proud of what you do and who you are. If you are a sales veteran, you are probably good at this already. If you're not there yet, with practice you will learn to turn your network and your investment in helping others into real dollars. Networking goes beyond befriending people; you have to turn those relationships into real business.

Getting the business

Building relationships exposes you to opportunities. The more people that know you, and that know that you are in the business of helping people buy and sell real estate, the better the chances are that you will discover more clients. If you have a large network and no one is helping you then it's not a network, it's a database. People who whine that they never get anything from networking are usually the ones who are networking with only their own needs in mind. Give before you receive.

We have encountered many agents who spend a lot of their money, time, and energy trying to cultivate new clients and referral sources. Instead, try working with the important existing relationships that you already have created. You

must remember that networking is not just about finding the next listing so that you can make more money; it's
about creating mutually beneficial relationships with others. If the only thing you do when you talk to others is ask
them if they know anyone who wants to buy or sell real
estate, then you are being selfish. Go deeper and discover
what the other person needs to be successful in their life,
too.

Show them how to help you

Never assume that someone is thinking about you and
your business, not even your nearest and dearest. There are
times when you need to ask the people you know for their
business or for a referral. Even people who frequently send
referrals your way deserve a reminder about how important they are to your success. People like to feel as if they
make a difference in the lives of others. The clearer you are
about how people can help you, the more likely they are
to do so. If you have invested enough in the relationship, it
should not be uncomfortable to have these discussions. If
you have given referrals to the other person, or found other ways to demonstrate that you bring value to them, they
will welcome your efforts to help them help you succeed.

Build internal support by sharing your network

Your network also extends into your agency and its other
real estate professionals. There are many advantages to

being seen as a resource by your colleagues. Find ways to build your internal network, teach others, help other agents succeed, and allow those in your company to tap into your external network. Done correctly, this can be good for the individuals you work with and for the success of your company. While real estate seems like a competitive industry, your co-workers are not the enemy. Find ways to ensure that everyone succeeds and you will see a higher level of success.

Sometimes your internal network will include individuals that do not have your best interests at heart, but whom you must deal with regularly. While there is no way to avoid office politics, you can stay out of it and try not to be brought down by it. Lead by example and always be the absolute picture of integrity. Become the Go-To Agent in your office and throughout your market. Others will admire you for it, and it will strengthen your reputation. No amount of money can buy a great reputation. Only your consistent actions over the long run will create your personal brand.

When you have a large network, be careful to not appear like you are just out on the cocktail party circuit having fun. People who do not understand the power of business networking think that attending seminars, giving speeches, and writing articles are merely egocentric activities. Done properly, however, your networking efforts are part of a long-term career strategy.

Bring people from your office to networking functions and help them make connections. Introducing coworkers to other people in your network will show them that you have their best interest at heart. Don't be afraid of others stealing your contacts; if you have established real friendships, nobody can take them away. Make sure that you are building your brand as well as your company's brand and you will always be safe.

Taking this a step further, one of the smartest things you can do is to introduce your higher-ups to those in your network. Many successful managers already have comprehensive lists of people with whom they have developed solid friendships over the years. However, all smart business professionals are interested in meeting additional key people in their community. If you know someone that your manager or team leader could benefit from knowing, facilitate the introduction. Doing so enables you to be viewed as an important company resource.

Never burn a bridge

How you say goodbye is just as important as how you say hello. When you decide to leave a company, a board on which you serve or another organization, consider your relationships with the people there. The reason for your departure may be positive, in which case it is easy to remain on good terms. This is the case when those you leave behind can clearly see that it is in your best interest and does not negatively impact their lives. Conversely, you might be severing your association ties because of negative reasons. You could be joining a competitor or leaving a volunteer position mid-term because of other obligations. If your departure will create challenges for those you leave behind, be extra cautious of what you say and how you treat the others. This can be a difficult situation, so taking the high road and expressing gratitude and appreciation helps.

People who join a competitor almost always try to take other agents with them. This can set up some ill will with your former employer who may feel threatened by your departure. Tread very cautiously. Never badmouth other agents or other brokers. Becoming the best that you can be does not mean putting down others to lift your own self up. Any time you say something negative about another person, know that it will get back to them. If you put it in an email, you can be sure that it will be forwarded to the people you are addressing. The best way to explain joining a competitor is to simply tell the world that you are excited by the new opportunity, and leave it at that.

The same is true if you leave a volunteer organization. Many people abandon their commitments if they get busy with work-related issues. The others to whom your responsibilities are shifted will not appreciate your departure, especially if you are negative about the organization or nonchalant about your departure. If you have to leave a volunteer position before you have completed your term, try to find others who can step in and complete your obligation. Even if the organization is not your highest priority, it is important to others. By belittling the organization, you are belittling those who dedicate their resources to it. One never knows when your paths will cross again.

CONCLUSION:
MAKING NETWORKING
WORK FOR YOU

People with large, functional networks understand that other people are a valuable resource. Like money in the bank that is both saved for a rainy day and pays interest, your network is important for both today's business and as an investment in your future.

Networking is an important component to a successful career in real estate. There are too many people in the business to only rely on the brand of your company and your knowledge of the neighborhoods where you represent clients. People in your community must know and like you on a personal level in order to send you a steady stream of referrals.

Every day in every city and town there are real estate agents finding new business because of their networking efforts. We hope that this book has helped you get beyond any preconceived notions that you might have had and inspired you to embrace the power of business relationships. When you put in the effort to help others and establish mutually beneficial long-term relationships you will create a way to keep your career prosperous in all economic conditions. Real estate will have booms and busts, but the agent who has positive interactions with a large network will always have clients.

Think of it this way: you can spend a ton of money sending out postcards to people you don't know and hope they call you. Or, you can dedicate yourself to building a strong group of connections that know and like you. It is not only a better way to build your business; it is more cost effective and fun. Savvy networking is something that is both natural and transparent. You come across as being friendly and interested in those around you. While it doesn't come easily to everyone, it can be learned using the basics in this book.

The results will not happen overnight, and you will not necessarily know when and where the payoff will occur, but success will follow those who are dedicated to the real cause of establishing a mutually beneficial network. The most successful networkers are the ones who keep at it and have fun along the way. You can do it, just like we have.

APPENDIX

RECOMMENDED READING

Bettinger, Frank. *How I Raised Myself from Failure to Success in Selling*. Prentice Hall Press, 1986.

Blanchard, Ken and, Sheldon Bowles. *Raving Fans*. William Morrow Company, Inc., 1993.

Godin, Seth. *Permission Marketing*. Simon and Schuster, 1999.

Hill, Napoleon. *Think and Grow Rich*. JMW Group, Tarcher Penguin Books, 2005.

Keller, Gary with Dave Jenks and Jay Papasan. *Shift*. Rellek Publishing Partners, Ltd, 2009.

Maxwell, John C. *The 21 Irrefutable Laws of Leadership*. Thomas Nelson Publishing, 2007.

Maxwell, John C and Les Parrott. *25 Ways To Win with People*. Thomas Nelson Publishing, 2005.

Misner, Ivan R. *The World's Best Known Marketing Secret*. Bard Press, 2007.

Mitchell, Jack. *Hug Your Customers*. Hyperion, 2003.

Ruiz, Don Miguel. *The Four Agreements*. Amber-Allen Publishing, Inc., 1997.

ABOUT THE AUTHORS

CHAD GOLDWASSER

Chad Goldwasser is the founder and CEO of Goldwasser International, a residential real estate firm in Austin, Texas.

In 2008, the Goldwasser team helped more than 400 families buy and sell real estate, and its sales volume exceeded $100 million. The team has won numerous honors for its achievements, including Realtor of the Year from the Austin Home Builders Association in 2005 and a number one ranking by the *Austin Business Journal* for 2007 and 2008. The company has also been recognized as one of the top 50 real estate teams by *Lore* magazine and the *Wall Street Journal*.

Chad is a popular public speaker who motivates and enriches lives through his talks about attitude, leadership, and personal growth. In 2007, he co-founded Right Course, a non-profit organization dedicated to helping single-parent families pay the costs for their children to participate in organized sports through the help of public, private, and corporate donations and grants.

Chad and his wife Tara are the parents of three young children and live in Austin.

Chad can be reached at chad@goldwasserrealestate.com

THOM SINGER

Thom Singer has two decades of experience in sales, marketing, and business development. He is experienced in branding, positioning, and networking, having worked with several Fortune 500 companies. He is a popular professional speaker, having trained over 20,000 professionals in the art of establishing meaningful connections that lead to increased business.

Thom has written six books on the power of business relationships and networking, and is a regular contributor to several industry publications.

Thom and his wife, Sara, make their home in Austin, Texas and are the parents of two highly spirited daughters. He is also the son of a successful real estate agent.

Thom can be reached at thom@thomsinger.com.